To Jamison, my friend and co-pastor, who leads with tenacity, overcomes setbacks with resilience, loves with a big heart, and seeks to outdo others in showing honor.

Table of Contents

Foreword — vi

Introduction: The Gospel for Defenders — 1

Day 1: The Struggle — 8

Day 2: A Return to Innocence — 12

Day 3: Nothing Left to Prove — 16

Day 4: Deborah Is a Boss — 20

Day 5: Flex Your Muscles — 24

Day 6: Jesus Is All In — 28

Day 7: Clothed with Power — 32

Day 8: Larger Than Life — 36

Day 9: The Cursing Psalms — 40

Day 10: Strength and Swagger — 44

Day 11: Taking Charge — 48

Day 12: The God Who Declares — 52

Day 13: Tap the Brakes — 56

Day 14: Confrontational Intimacy — 60

Day 15: Scalpel over Sledgehammer — 64

Day 16: Conflict Activators — 68

Day 17: Nebuchadnezzar's Narcissism — 72

Day 18: Thriving at Work — 76

Day 19: Authority over Anarchy — 80

Day 20: Lust for Intensity — 84

Day 21: Love Has a Backbone — 88

Praise for
The Gospel for Defenders

"Honest and insightful, winsome and wise, encouraging and challenging, soul-nourishing, and heart-warming! Most importantly, over the course of a 40-day journey, this little gem invites me into spaces of gospel-suffused vulnerability and spiritual intimacy with Christ. Gritty and grace-filled, I can't say enough about this devotional guide!"
— **Todd Wilson, PhD, co-founder of the Center for Pastor Theologians and author of** *The Enneagram Goes to Church: Wisdom for Leadership, Worship, and Congregational Life*

"Jeff and I are thankful the Lord has provided more gospel-centered Enneagram teachers like Tyler Zach. Whether you are new to the Enneagram or have studied it for years, we know that you'll find lasting value in this book. On these pages, Tyler's creative wisdom shines, and his focus always remains on Jesus."
— **Beth & Jeff McCord, co-founders of Your Enneagram Coach, best-selling authors of** *Becoming Us: Using the Enneagram to Create a Thriving Gospel-Centered Marriage*

"Equally convincing and liberating, this masterful guide is one that every Type Eight needs on their journey of sanctification."
— **Meredith Boggs, author of** *The Journey Home: A Biblical Guide to Using the Enneagram to Deepen Your Faith and Relationships*

" ... A personalized devotional for your personality type. I love it! ... "
— **Les Parrott, PhD, #1** *New York Times* **bestselling author of** *Saving Your Marriage Before It Starts*

" ... an extraordinary gift to all Enneagram enthusiasts ... "
— **Marilyn Vancil, author of** *Self to Lose, Self to Find: Using the Enneagram to Uncover Your True, God-Gifted Self*

" ... Journey through these pages to remember who you are and how to bring your best self to a world in need. ... "

— **Drew Moser, PhD, author of *The Enneagram of Discernment: The Way of Vocation, Wisdom, and Practice***

" ... clear, compelling, and beyond profound."

— **John Fooshee, president of *People Launching and Gospel Enneagram***

The Gospel for Defenders

A 40-Day Devotional for
Powerful, Challenging Protectors

BY TYLER ZACH

The Gospel for Defenders: A 40-Day Devotional for Powerful, Challenging Protectors: (Enneagram Type 8)

© 2023 by Tyler Zach

Edited by Joshua Casey, Stephanie Cross, and Lee Ann Roberts

All rights reserved. No part of this publication may be reproduced, stored in a retrieval system, or transmitted in any form or by any means, electronic, mechanical, photocopying, recording or otherwise—except for brief quotations in critical reviews or articles, without the prior written permission of the author.

To request permission, contact the author at tyler@gospelforenneagram.com.

Unless otherwise indicated, all Scripture quotations are from the ESV® Bible (The Holy Bible, English Standard Version®), copyright © 2001 by Crossway, a publishing ministry of Good News Publishers. Used by permission. All rights reserved.

Scripture quotations marked (NIV) are taken from the Holy Bible, New International Version®, NIV®. Copyright © 1973, 1978, 1984, 2011 by Biblica, Inc.® Used by permission of Zondervan. All rights reserved worldwide. www.zondervan.com The "NIV" and "New International Version" are trademarks registered in the United States Patent and Trademark Office by Biblica, Inc.™

Scripture quotations marked (NLT) are taken from the Holy Bible, New Living Translation, copyright ©1996, 2004, 2007, 2013, 2015 by Tyndale House Foundation. Used by permission of Tyndale House Publishers, Inc., Carol Stream, IL 60188. All rights reserved.

Cover design by Fruitful Design (www.fruitful.design)
Interior Design and eBook by Kelley Creative

ISBN: 979-8-870925-39-4

www.gospelforenneagram.com

Day 22: Blind Spots in Love	92
Day 23: My Way Or the Highway	96
Day 24: Navigating Denial	100
Day 25: The Strong Shepherd	104
Day 26: Lion and the Lamb	108
Day 27: Knockout Punch	112
Day 28: The Loneliness of Leadership	116
Day 29: Betrayed with a Kiss	120
Day 30: The Volcano of Emotions	124
Day 31: Facing Grief	128
Day 32: It's Demo Day!	132
Day 33: BS Detector	136
Day 34: The Illusion of Invincibility	140
Day 35: Rising Above Revenge	144
Day 36: No Mercy	148
Day 37: Mafia Leaders	152
Day 38: Trust Issues	156
Day 39: Making the Impossible Possible	160
Day 40: Eightness Is Greatness	164
Prayer for Defenders	168
Three Types of Defenders	169
Next Steps	172
Acknowledgements	173

Foreword

When Jeff and I first discovered the Enneagram, it wasn't easy finding books written from a Christian worldview. We understood how important gospel-centered Enneagram resources could be, and that inspired us to start our business, Your Enneagram Coach. Since then, we've helped over one million people find their Type through our free assessment and grow through our online classes, coaching certifications, books, and podcast.

Type Eights are assertive, self-confident, and big-hearted. They engage in life fully with passion, intensity, and strength. Their determination to make things happen makes them powerful change agents in the world, especially when seeking justice and protection for others. I've had the joy of working with several Eights. Under their leadership, our business reached new levels of success and creativity.

The Enneagram is a tool that clarifies our fallen nature while also reminding us that we are created in the imago Dei (image of God). When Jeff and I understood the why behind our thoughts and actions, it transformed how we looked at ourselves, our relationship with God, our marriage, our parenting, and (obviously) our careers. Taking a risk by starting a business was both exciting and terrifying. We could have easily spun out of control or run out of gas (at times, we did!), but knowing the Enneagram, as seen through the lens of the gospel, kept us grounded and on track.

The world needs Eights because your instinctive intuition sees possibilities others overlook. You're never afraid to say what needs to be said to ensure people receive justice. Like Christ, you are courageous and help others find their strength. You plow a path to overcome obstacles for the benefit of many.

Like all numbers, Eights have seasons of struggle. Underneath your outward strength is a tender heart with a deep fear of betrayal. You hide your heart behind thick armor, but inevitably, this self-protection ends up doing more harm than good. When you sacrifice intimacy, you miss out on the connection and support for which you were created. A gospel-centered Enneagram can help you see that vulnerability is a sign of strength, not weakness. Eights, this 40-day devotional will guide you to the true freedom you desire so you can put down your armor and find rest.

Jeff and I are thankful the Lord has provided more gospel-centered Enneagram teachers like Tyler Zach. Whether you are new to the Enneagram or have studied it for years, we know you'll find lasting value in this book. On these pages, Tyler's creative wisdom shines, and his focus always remains on Jesus. We're praying God will meet you on these pages, and you will recognize your inherent value as His beloved child.

Jesus is the author and perfecter of our faith (Hebrews 12:2). He finished the great task He set out to accomplish (John 19:30). A vital part of His ministry was to stay in alignment with His Father, and He did this by setting aside time for rest and reflection. He invites you to do the same—to come away, to separate from the crowds and be with Him. Remember, you are loved and valued for simply being you. You do not have to gain Christ's approval. You are accepted right now as you are.

—Beth and Jeff McCord
co-founders of Your Enneagram Coach
best-selling authors of *Becoming Us: Using the Enneagram to Create a Thriving Gospel-Centered Marriage* and *More Than Your Number: A Christ-Centered Enneagram Approach to Becoming AWARE of Your Internal World*

Introduction:
The Gospel for Defenders

IT'S GO TIME!

Welcome to *The Gospel for Defenders*: an in-depth window into your personality type. I promise you that this book is not one of those devotionals filled with inspiring fluff that will make you roll your eyes. Nor is it a pep talk that will get you fired up for a few hours while still avoiding the root problems in your life. Think of this book as a 40-day "rock tumbler" that will refine those rough edges without compromising your true self.

Speaking of being a rock, you're not just a reliable anchor for us during our tough times but a fierce protector—a bear guarding its cubs. You're the general who leads us fearlessly into the battle; the seasoned sea captain who navigates the stormy waters of conflict. When life turns cold and desolate, you're the roaring flame that warms us all. If you were a key on a keyboard, you'd undoubtedly be the exclamation mark, consistently grabbing our attention when God wants to deliver a message.

For the next 40 days, I'm here to walk alongside you, offering honest guidance to unleash your power and elevate your leadership and relationships. Inside these pages lie challenges that'll push you like never before, perhaps even stirring a few tears. My goal is neither to flatter nor anger you but to offer genuine words of affirmation and challenge from your heavenly Defender, who intentionally created you just the way you are.

Have you ever felt taken aback by how people perceive you, wondering, *Why do they think I'm always ready for a fight?* You've been a challenger since the womb, and not everyone gets that. But guess what? God does. He understands that you are one of the most misinterpreted personalities out there.

Your unwavering confidence is often misinterpreted and not always appreciated, even if you do seem to rise faster than others up the chain of command and earn everyone's respect. Even I, at times, have confused your self-assurance as pride—especially as someone on the other end of the spectrum who struggles with false humility. But what I once saw as your weakness, I now see as your greatest asset. That's why I chose the title "Defender" over "Challenger"—the tired moniker most Enneagram teachers use for this type—because it is truly your *strengths* that define you above all else.

What Makes This Book Different?

While other books explain the Enneagram, this book's primary aim is to go deeper by applying the truth of God's Word specifically to your type over the next 40 days. If you are suspicious of the Enneagram or know someone who is, download my free resource called *Should Christians Use the Enneagram?* at gospelforenneagram.com. I pray it will help you engage with this system as a Christian and then talk about it with others.

Before we get to the daily devotions, let's look at how the gospel both affirms and challenges the unique characteristics of your type.

The Gospel Affirms Defenders

God sympathizes with the worldview of a Defender. This unfair and apathetic world lacks justice in many ways, and is filled with oppressors, cowards, and chronic critics. We need strong, passionate doers who will empower us to reject apathy, lead courageously, protect fiercely, and overcome adversity. Your life is our daily reminder that "faith apart from works is dead."[1] All Defenders will be happy to know the Bible affirms the following beliefs:

- **God created us to be strong and courageous.** "Have I not commanded you? Be strong and courageous. Do not be frightened, and do not be dismayed, for the LORD your God is with you wherever you go."[2]

---

1 James 2:26

2 Joshua 1:9

- **God created us to be doers who take initiative.** "But be doers of the word, and not hearers only, deceiving yourselves."[3]

- **God created us to seek justice and protect the vulnerable.** "Learn to do good; seek justice, correct oppression; bring justice to the fatherless, plead the widow's cause."[4]

- **God created us to work hard and never give up.** "And let us not grow weary of doing good, for in due season we will reap, if we do not give up."[5]

- **God created us to be direct and decisive.** "Let what you say be simply 'Yes' or 'No'; anything more than this comes from evil."[6]

- **God created us to be victorious conquerors.** "No, in all these things we are more than conquerors through him who loved us."[7]

- **God created us to be righteously angry.** "Be angry and sin … ."[8]

- **God created us to live with passion.** "Do not be slothful in zeal, be fervent in spirit, serve the Lord."[9]

The Gospel Challenges Defenders

The gospel also provides specific challenges to Defenders. We'll explore the most common lies Eights believe and see how the Bible provides much better promises and blessings. We will move deeper into each of these throughout the next 40 days.

- **Lie #1: I'm loved for being strong and tough.** Eights are a gift to the world, displaying God's *power and strength*.[10] However, this role gets exaggerated when they believe they will only be respected or loved when they are strong enough

---

3 James 1:22
4 Isaiah 1:17
5 Galatians 6:9
6 Matthew 5:37
7 Romans 8:37
8 Ephesians 4:26a
9 Romans 12:11
10 Marilyn Vancil, *Self to Lose Self to Find: Using the Enneagram to Uncover Your True, God-gifted Self* (New York: Convergent, 2020), 98.

to be feared. But the truth is: Jesus died on the cross for your *vulnerable* self, not your invincible self. This book is a call to put down your weapons, take off your armor, and return to the Eight's core virtue of childlike *innocence*. When you fall into the arms of your Father and Defender, you'll receive protection from all your enemies, mercy for all your guilt, and finally realize there's nothing left to prove. He couldn't be more proud of you right now.

- **Lie #2: Vulnerability is a sign of weakness.** Living in a world where the strong eat the weak, Eights avoid *vulnerability* at all costs to protect themselves and garner respect. They tend to not tolerate any weakness in themselves or others, confuse vulnerability for weakness, and deny their softer emotions. Eights must embrace the truth that becoming vulnerable paradoxically makes you stronger, not weaker. After all, Jesus is *both* the Lion and the Lamb, proving that becoming more tender doesn't make you less tough. Embracing vulnerability and transparency will only develop your emotional intelligence, giving you the ability to understand and manage your feelings and making you a more approachable friend, lover, and leader.

- **Lie #3: Bigger is better.** The vice of an Eight is *lust*. Much more than sexual interest, it is a *desire for intensity* in all of life. Eights work hard and play hard. They want to squeeze the most out of every moment, which may lead them to over-do everything and become the proverbial bull in a china shop, causing them to burn out or burn bridges. The truth is that, more often than not, less is more and bigger is not always better. Living without limits is what's actually limiting you. Therefore, God places boundaries around your passion for intensity, not because He's a kill-joy, but because He wants to protect your pleasure. Spreading yourself too thin or putting your relationships on thin ice actually jeopardizes your potential joy, so tap the brakes and embrace rest as renewal rather than an inconvenience.

- **Lie #4: I will be betrayed.** The core fears of an Eight are being *controlled, harmed, or betrayed*. Their childhood message was: It's not okay to trust or be vulnerable with others. This explains why many Eights have trust issues and rely solely on themselves. Some may constantly test and challenge others, trying to uncover hidden motives, but this approach only results in increased loneliness or low-grade paranoia. The good news is that Jesus, who experienced rejection and betrayal from both His enemies and closest friends, says, "I will never betray you."[11] Knowing you are safe in Christ will lead you to live with open hands rather than closed fists, knowing there are people who are ready to love you fiercely when you have the courage to let them in.

- **Lie #5: I must take justice into my own hands.** When the Eight's fear of betrayal comes true, or they witness a bully misusing their power, they may take action, believing every battle is theirs to fight or that it is their sole responsibility to balance the scales. Because the Eight's fixation is *vengeance*, they may believe that revenge works, but mercy will only invite further exploitation. However, taking on the role of the vigilante will only continue the cycle of hostility and violence in the world, blocking our path to reconciliation and understanding. Just as it was God's kindness, not vengeance, that led you to repentance,[12] so you must seek to forgive rather than repay. Forgiveness demands greater courage than punishment, but it's the only way to set you free from the chains of anger and bitterness that can hold you captive for years.

- **Lie #6: No one can tell me what to do.** As autonomous and independent creatures, Eights want to stay in control of their present environment and future destiny. They may suffer from the illusion of invincibility, believing they are more powerful than the rest of us weaklings and aren't bound by the same human limitations. The Eight's defense mechanism is *denial*, which leads them to dismiss inconvenient truths that don't fit into their way of seeing things, but they must swallow the pill that excessive self-confidence can actually derail their vision. The solution is to trust in the Lord and not lean on your own understanding,[13] considering yourself a "fool" rather than "wise" in your own eyes.[14] The path to greatness and leaving an unforgettable legacy involves surrendering your willfulness to God's will, allowing yourself to decrease so that He may increase.[15]

As you can see, the gospel will challenge your perception of the protagonists and antagonists in your life. In the Defender's Kingdom, the world is divided into "the

---

11 Matthew 28:20, author's paraphrase
12 Romans 2:4
13 Proverbs 3:5-6
14 1 Corinthians 3:18
15 John 3:30

strong" and "the weak": your heroes are those who stand up for themselves and prove to be tough, extremely loyal, fully committed, truthful, and resilient. They also don't try to get in your way, giving you all the autonomy and independence you think you need. Conversely, your villains are those who undermine your decisions, act subversively behind your back or try to catch you off-guard; they persistently challenge your authority, try to manipulate or control you, or portray you as the "angry bad guy."

God's kingdom will not be filled with those who use Christ's authority as an excuse to fight their enemies but by men and women who have learned to forgive. In God's economy, *mercy is the currency*. In this place, we exchange guilt for grace, ego for empathy, suspicion for trust, dominance for exercising dominion, and we embrace the reality that might doesn't always make right. Here, we prioritize *feeling* before doing, *listening* before acting prematurely, and acknowledge that true fulfillment is not found in powering up but in the presence of God.[16]

The Invitation

When Jesus Christ, the divine all in all, entered into flawed and limited human history, He started His mission with an invitation: "The time is fulfilled, and the kingdom of God is at hand; repent and believe in the gospel."[17] He explained that to enter the good, eternally renewing life that begins well before the grave, you must do two things: believe the truth and turn from sin. "Believing" includes acknowledging who God is, who He says we are, and what He has done for us. More than that, to truly believe in a Christlike way is to *actively live into* those acknowledgments. "Turning" includes shedding our false worldview, misplaced desires, strong defenses, hide-and-seek strategies, and self-salvation efforts.

If you are ready to begin this incredible 40-day journey and accept God's invitation, then let's go! It will be an enlightening ride of rapid growth as you become more self-aware and experience newfound freedom. You will encounter many light-bulb moments as you read profound truths for your type—and maybe even learn something about the people around you. The things you learn about yourself in this book will stick with you for the rest of your life.

---

16 Scott Loughrige, Clare M. Loughrige, Douglas A. Calhoun, and Adele Ahlberg Calhoun, *Spiritual Rhythms For The Enneagram: A Handbook for Harmony and Transformation* (Downers Grove, IL: InterVarsity Press, 2019), 21.

17 Mark 1:15

Three Types of Defenders

To further explore how Eights can look very different from one another, please check out the "Three Types of Defenders" in the back of this book. These "subtypes" are helpful in understanding the nuances of the Defender, and will explain why some truths in this devotional will hit home more than others. If you are a Social Eight for example, you will often look a lot more like a Two, but if you are a Self-Preservation Eight, you will look more Five-ish. These descriptions are meant to help you further uncover the unconscious motivations driving your behavior and may even help you discover why you're often confused with other Enneagram types!

A Note About Female Eights

Female Eights face tough challenges as their assertive nature often clashes with conventional gender expectations. While men are commonly applauded for being strong and aggressive leaders, women are often labeled the "b" word for displaying the same qualities and might feel pressured to conform to traditional expectations of womanhood, such as being warm, nurturing, and flexible.

Some of my friends have expressed that they don't resonate with typical Eight descriptions. For instance, Eights are often labeled as domineering, but due to cultural (and especially church) norms, many Eight women have never been granted leadership roles, given permission to speak, or compensated for their gifts. It's imperative that we work harder to acknowledge these biases and actively foster an environment that values the strengths of all female Eights. With their leadership, we will have more role models, diverse perspectives, a more full understanding of spiritual teachings, better decision-making, and greater advocacy for marginalized groups. We *need* them—*you*—now more than ever!

Day 1:
The Struggle

They will make war on the Lamb, and the Lamb will conquer them, for he is Lord of lords and King of kings, and those with him are called and chosen and faithful.

—Revelation 17:14

LIFE CAN BE A STRUGGLE, FIERCE AND unrelenting, with many obstacles and foes. It tests our strength and often strains our spirit. Sometimes life feels like a relentless grind, but that doesn't stop you from dreaming impossible dreams. Through hardship and shattered expectations, Defenders always seem able to dip into untapped sources of strength, pivot, and find a way to make a fresh start. As Nietzsche said, the struggle doesn't kill you but only makes you stronger.[2] Eights are the epitome of those who "are afflicted in every way, but not crushed; perplexed, but not driven to despair; persecuted, but not forsaken; struck down, but not destroyed."[3]

> If there is no struggle, there is no progress.
> —Frederick Douglass[1]

---

1   Frederick Douglass, *Narrative of the Life of Frederick Douglass and Other Works* (San Diego, CA: Canterbury Classics, 2014).

2   Tudury, Leila. "What Doesn't Kill You, Makes You Stronger Meaning & Origin." Dictionary.com, January 19, 2021. https://www.dictionary.com/e/slang/what-doesnt-kill-you-makes-you-stronger/.

3   2 Corinthians 4:8-9

Yet, let's pause for a moment and consider the perspective of the Defender without God. In that mindset, Defenders become Terminators, scanning the world for enemies—and they are seldom disappointed. They view the world through the lens of scarcity—a cold, hostile, threatening place where the strong eat the weak, the powerful take advantage of others, and no one gets a break. In this world, they must do whatever they can to survive, fending for themselves and taking whatever they can get. In this world, most people have bad intentions and cannot be trusted. As psychologist Dr. Jerry Wagner says, average to unhealthy Eights "come into a situation with a chip on their shoulder, looking for opposition, anticipating a fight, and expecting to be taken advantage of."[4]

While many may find this is a dark and depressing view of the world, it is also true that both oppressors and victims live in our world. There are those whose negative experiences, untended trauma, and illnesses drive them to inflict pain on those around them—a motif explored in countless westerns, crime dramas, war stories, and mobster movies. Even many Biblical stories show the brutal capacity of humanity without pulling any punches.

> Through Jesus' death and resurrection, the Eight's yearning for vindictive triumph finds fulfillment.

Your realist view of the world serves you well—as well as those you protect. Consider this: if Harriet Tubman or Martin Luther King, Jr. hadn't seen the world through the lens of an Eight, the Underground Railroad and Civil Rights Movement both would have looked very different. Contrary to what some might believe, the world isn't always rosy, filled with rainbows, butterflies, and unicorns. It is a struggle of good against evil, with a spiritual enemy who seeks to devour us.[5] And we choose every day whether to bring heaven or hell to bear on the tiny piece of the world we touch.

As an Eight, you have the ability to put on redemptive lenses and recognize that with the right leverage, the world can just as easily become a place of beauty,

---

[4] Jerome Peter Wagner, *Nine Lenses on the World: The Enneagram Perspective* (Evanston, IL: NineLens Press, 2010), 415.

[5] 1 Peter 5:8

joy, and love, where you can extend trust to others. When you choose to submit to God's protection, you can learn to become tender and vulnerable without constantly fearing harm and realize that not everyone who disagrees with you is your enemy.

The Good News for Defenders is Jesus understands the struggle intimately. He is the Suffering Servant who experienced hatred, rejection, mockery, and betrayal from enemies and even His closest friends. He knows what it's like to be a prophetic leader and change agent, yet not receive honor within His own hometown[6]—just as you may not always be respected or embraced within your own family, church, denomination, or tribe.

But through Jesus' death and resurrection, the Eight's yearning for vindictive triumph finds fulfillment. Although the cross initially appeared as a failure, as if Jesus had been overcome, the game was not over. The book of Revelation reveals the ultimate triumph of the Lamb, the King of kings and Lord of lords, who will conquer all enemies of peace and flourishing through His sacrificial love. Those who have bowed their knees to King Jesus will be able to claim His victory as their own.

Don't give up, because soon you will bask in glory, receiving a crown for your unwavering perseverance through life's fiery trials.[7] When Jesus returns, He will declare you chosen and faithful.

→ Pray

Father, help me to release my defensive posture and embrace the redemptive lenses You offer amid life's struggles, seeing beauty and love everywhere I go. Thank You for the transformative power of Your presence and the victory found in Jesus' victory over Satan, sin, and death. Give me perseverance to endure and be counted as chosen and faithful when Jesus returns.

---

6   Matthew 13:57

7   James 1:12

Day 1 Reflections:

How does the perspective of being "afflicted in every way, but not crushed; perplexed, but not driven to despair; persecuted, but not forsaken; struck down, but not destroyed" resonate with your experiences in life?

_____
_____
_____

Reflect on the tendency to approach situations with a defensive posture, anticipating opposition and expecting to be taken advantage of. How has this mindset impacted your interactions with others?

_____
_____
_____

Consider the balance between recognizing the harsh realities of the world and embracing the beauty, joy, and love that exist. How can you cultivate a redemptive lens that acknowledges both aspects?

_____
_____
_____

> ### → Respond
>
> Search for, listen to, and meditate on the song "Eight" from the Sleeping At Last project, Atlas: II.

Day 2:
A Return to Innocence

And they were bringing children to him that he might touch them, and the disciples rebuked them. But when Jesus saw it, he was indignant and said to them, "Let the children come to me; do not hinder them, for to such belongs the kingdom of God. Truly, I say to you, whoever does not receive the kingdom of God like a child shall not enter it."

—Mark 10:13-15

MANY YEARS AGO, IN A HOSPITAL ROOM filled with anticipation and joy, a miracle of life unfolded before everyone's eyes. The air was thick with excitement as loved ones gathered, their faces beaming with pure delight as a mother, exhausted but euphoric, cradled the tiny bundle in her arms. With each delicate breath, the newborn filled the room with innocence. The baby, oblivious to the

> Vulnerability sounds like truth and feels like courage. Truth and courage aren't always comfortable, but they're never weakness.
>
> –Brené Brown[1]

---

1 Drew Moser, *The Enneagram of Discernment: The Way of Vocation, Wisdom, and Practice* (Beaver Falls, PA: Falls City Press, 2020), 168.

world's expectations, had yet to utter a word or accomplish any grand feat, but in this moment, surrounded by smiles and tears, love and admiration were heaped on them in their most vulnerable and helpless state.

That little child was once *you*. Take a moment to consider: At your smallest and least "accomplished," other humans stood near and rejoiced at the mere fact of your existence. You are not merely the child of your parents, though. You are first and foremost a beloved child of God; a being that brings the Divine unspeakable joy simply for existing and being yourself.

But here's the rub: like all parents love their kids more than they need them, God loves you more than He needs you. You may have grown accustomed to nearly everyone leaning on you because you are tough and courageous, but those aren't the reasons you are cherished. When you internalize this truth, you can finally return to *innocence*, the core virtue for all Eights. Innocence is difficult for an Eight to reclaim later in life because they often feel they had to grow up too quickly to protect themselves and their loved ones, resulting in the faulty belief that it is better to be feared than loved.

> God loves you more than He needs you.

Author Merdith Boggs, an Eight herself, explains in her own words that "innocence is a state of being unstained and unhindered by sin, free from all the pain and struggle that accumulates over a lifetime. It's the initial innocence of the garden, where Adam and Eve dwelt in Eden and communed with God, unencumbered by their vices, unashamed of their nakedness and vulnerability."[2] The Latin root for innocence is *innocens*, which means "harmless."[3] Innocent people are those who carry the attitude of "Why would I want to hurt anyone? And why would anyone want to hurt me?"[4]

Jesus once told His disciples, "whoever does not receive the kingdom of God like a child shall not enter it,"[5] stressing to His disciples that one must come to God

---

[2] Meredith Boggs, *The Journey Home: A Biblical Guide to Using the Enneagram to Deepen Your Faith and Relationships* (Nashville, TN: Thomas Nelson, 2023), 44.

[3] Innocence (n.). Etymology. Accessed November 15, 2023. https://www.etymonline.com/word/innocence.

[4] Wagner, *Nine Lenses on the World*, 411-412.

[5] Mark 10:15

with unabashed curiosity and openness, and unashamedly helpless, defenseless, and without merit—as opposed to approaching with certainty, strength, and swagger. Those who possess these childlike qualities will also possess the kingdom of God. The audacity of a child's innocence eclipses the might of a grown man or woman's strength.

Jesus is neither naive nor asking you to be, for He later told His disciples, "I am sending you out like sheep among wolves. Therefore be as shrewd as snakes and as innocent as doves."[6] Here He calls them to pair shrewdness—which all Eights appear to possess quite naturally—with innocence, something that needs to be *re*possessed.

So, what does cultivating innocence (or "harmlessness") look like, practically? Like a baby who forgets about the pain right after it goes away, innocence means not allowing past hurts to cause distrust in new relationships. It means slowing down enough to pay attention to your heart, helping you become more sensitive. It means putting your weapons down *first*, approaching others with vulnerability and openness, letting go of your need to judge them, and releasing your death grip on always wanting to control the situation.[7]

The Good News for Defenders is that Jesus entered into the world the same way as you. Though the Jews were longing for a fierce and strong Messiah, He came as a humble, vulnerable baby. The three wise men traveled from afar to bow to and bestow honor on a Child who would never pick up a sword or shield in battle. Jesus demonstrates that it takes far greater courage to hold onto innocence than rely on strength. Only the bravest hearts show their vulnerability. So let your strength and innocence entwine, allowing the latter to soften, heal, and transform the former so that your warrior's face is a true reflection of the King of kings.

---

6   Matthew 10:16 NIV

7   Beatrice Chestnut and Uranio Paes, *The Enneagram Guide to Waking Up: Find Your Path, Face Your Shadow, Discover Your True Self* (Charlottesville, VA: Hampton Roads Publishing, 2021), 229-230.

→ Pray

Father, fill me with the audacity of a child's innocence and guide me to cultivate harmlessness in my relationships. Teach me to let go of past hurts, listen to my heart, and be sensitive to others. Give me strength to lay down my weapons and release my need for control. Thank You for showing me that true courage lies in reaching for innocence.

Day 2 Reflections:

When have you experienced being loved and valued without being needed, just as the newborn in the story? How did that experience make you feel?

_____
_____
_____

How have your past experiences and the need to protect yourself affected your ability to embrace innocence?

_____
_____
_____

Reflect on the qualities of innocence exhibited by a child. How can you reconnect with those qualities in your own life? What do you need to let go of to reclaim your innocence?

_____
_____
_____

→ Respond

Write a letter to yourself expressing your deepest fears and vulnerabilities, allowing yourself to be completely honest and open.

Day 3:

Nothing Left to Prove

So God created man in his own image, in the image of God

he created him; male and female he created them.

—Genesis 1:27

THE RENOWNED AMERICAN NOVELIST ERNEST HEMINGWAY (1899–1961) shattered the mold of a reserved, scarf-clad artist. Even in his time, he was known as a certified badass, often referred to as "angrier than God on a bad day."[1] Hemingway believed that you should have both compassion and the ability to block punches.[2] He showed his courage once by leaping onto a bull's back, narrowly escaping injury. His valor extended to World War I, where he saved lives through fearless actions. As an ambulance driver, he endured a mortar shell blast, reportedly using brandy to numb the pain as he extracted shrapnel from his body at night.[3] Recognizing his gallantry,

> We are each of us like a small mirror in which God searches for His reflection.
>
> –St. John Vianney

---

1 Richard Rohr and Andreas Ebert, *The Enneagram: A Christian Perspective* (New York, NY: The Crossroad Publishing Company, 2001), 170-171.

2 Ibid., 170-171.

3 Ibid., 170-171.

the Italian government awarded him the Silver Medal of Military Valor for rescuing Italian soldiers during an attack.[4]

You can see many of the personality characteristics of an Eight in Hemingway (and even in many of his main literary characters).[5] Do you realize that we can see the traits of God more clearly through your Eightness? God created all of us as "mirrors" in His image to reflect different aspects of His heart and character to a broken, hurting world. When walking in the Spirit, you are just, merciful, protecting, compassionate, courageous, resilient, direct, self-confident, assertive, influential, and empowering.

Pause for a moment and read that list again. You are a remarkable reflection of God's power and strength.[6]

According to author Marilyn Vancil, Eights long to experience the aliveness of the original human state, the vitality of God's greatness, and the weight of His glory. Their deepest longing is to express the divine gift of power and might for the protection of others. As one Eight shared, "I feel most connected to God when I'm operating like a hose connected to a spigot—when His forcefulness flows through me to others. I sense His strength and know I'm being used for His purposes. I want to be aligned with God's passion for people and exercise my leadership gifts to stand with the helpless and provide opportunities for them to grow and reach their full potential. There is nothing quite as exhilarating as witnessing someone rise above their difficult circumstances and accomplish something they never dreamed they could."[7]

> You are a remarkable reflection of God's power and strength.

But as you know, it's impossible to reflect those characteristics of God at all times. The apostle Paul said the mirror was cracked from top to bottom when we exchanged the glory of God for the glory of man[8]—a mistake not just relegated

---

4   Kenneth S. Lynn, *Hemingway* (Cambridge, MA: Harvard University Press, 1995), 80.

5   Rohr and Ebert, *The Enneagram*, 170-171.

6   Vancil, *Self to Lose Self to Find*, 98.

7   Ibid., 98.

8   Romans 1:23

to people of the past but one we all make. The mirror was not cracked in some distant past but in our every moment of failure to live up to Christ's reflection. When walking in the flesh, those positive attributes turn sour, and you will find yourself being forceful, excessive, non-listening, intimidating, insensitive, domineering, rebellious, confrontational, possessive, threatening, or vengeful.

When you drift from the gospel promise that you are worthy because of Christ, you will work hard to prove yourself by picking up the chisel and carving the perfect "powerful" persona. Like ancient kings who put their faces on coins and statutes in order to project power, an unhealthy Eight strives to be omnipotent like God, making their imprint on their sphere of influence.[9] But this forceful image is not just about proving yourself; it's about protection. Like Adam and Eve, when feeling the awful sensation of being naked and vulnerable, you too are tempted to sew fig leaves together that say: "I am powerful and protected; I won't be neglected or taken advantage of."[10]

The Good News for Defenders is Jesus died on the cross for *you*—for your vulnerable self, not your invincible self. You are not worthy because you are a protector and provider. Rather, you are, right now without any effort, the *imago Dei*. The Holy Spirit is working like a master sculptor to clear away the excess marble and reveal what God sees: that tender heart beneath the tough image you work so hard to present to others. When God gazes into your mirror, He sees the image of His Son radiating back at Him, and He declares, "There's nothing left for you to prove."

→ Pray

Father, forgive me for striving to earn love and respect by carving out a persona of strength or power. May Your Holy Spirit continue to transform me, revealing the tender heart beneath the tough exterior I often present. Help me embrace the truth that my worthiness comes from Christ alone, not from proving how strong I can be for myself or others.

---

9   Don Riso and Russ Hudson, *Personality Types: Using the Enneagram for Self-Discovery* (New York, NY: Houghton Mifflin Company Books, 1996), 316.

10 Wagner, *Nine Lenses on the World*, 439.

Day 3 Reflections:

Which of these words most reflect the image of God in you: just, merciful, protecting, compassionate, courageous, resilient, direct, self-confident, assertive, influential, or empowering?

When did you start to believe the lie, "I'm more loved and respected when I'm strong"? What people or life experiences have reinforced that belief?

Where in your life are you trying to prove yourself to others? How can you let go of that striving and find rest in knowing you are beloved?

→ Respond

Commit to regularly sharing your vulnerabilities or weaknesses with someone in your life where you can drop the tough facade.

Day 4:

Deborah Is a Boss

*And Deborah said to Barak, "Up! For this is the day in which the L*ORD* has given Sisera into your hand. Does not the Lord go out before you?"*

—Judges 4:14a

DEBORAH, THE RENOWNED OLD TESTAMENT JUDGE, WARRIOR, poet, and prophet, exemplified the qualities of an Eight. In a time when female leaders with her level of authority were rare, Deborah rose to prominence. She identified herself as "a mother in Israel"[2] and embraced her role as a protector of the people. Like many Eights, Deborah took charge daily, making swift decisions with limited support or guidance, and had a passion for executing justice. As she took her seat of judgment under the palm tree between

> People lionize men who "kick ass and take names." Sadly, we all know the word people use to describe a woman in the workplace or the community who takes charge.
>
> –Ian Cron and Suzanne Stabile[1]

---

1 Ian Morgan Cron and Suzanne Stabile, *The Road Back to You* (Downers Grove, IL: InterVarsity Press Books, 2016), 57.

2 Judges 5:7

Ramah and Bethel, the Israelites lined up for her to rule on matters great and small because they trusted her wisdom.³

One day, she summoned Barak, the commander of Israel's army, and questioned why he had not taken action against their enemies, despite receiving a clear command from the Lord. Eights have little patience for those who cannot make decisions or lack commitment. But we can hardly blame Barak as he was up against a formidable king who held both numerical and technological advantages over the Israelites.

As the defender of her people, Deborah assumed leadership, publicly challenging her fellow countryman, admonishing him to obey the Lord's command. Rather than taking the reins herself and going around Barak, Deborah empowered him to do his job by giving him a public opportunity to fulfill his duty to protect Israel. After Barak contemplated her challenge, he came back with one condition: he would only proceed if Deborah accompanied him.⁴

> You are someone we can trust to help us overcome our obstacles and lead us to victory.

Deborah granted Barak's request but cautioned him that the glory of the victory would be attributed to a woman rather than to him. Already defying cultural norms, Deborah prepared him that this military triumph could be somewhat awkward for him,⁵ but with that out of the way, the army and its two leaders got to witness the Lord's glorious victory over their oppressive enemy. Following a battlefield rout, Deborah's prophetic word came true. After the enemy commander Sisera fled on foot from battle, he asked to hide in the tent of another woman named Jael. This extraordinary person gave the enemy commander a glass of milk and a bed. Then, as he slept, she ruthlessly drove a tent peg through his skull.⁶

---

3   Judges 4:4-5
4   Judges 4:6-8
5   Judges 4:9
6   Judges 4:17-22

Following this triumph, Deborah remained humble and, displaying the Eight's virtue of tenderness, engaged in a creative songwriting session with Barak, and together they sang a hymn of victory which you can read in Judges chapter 5. Ultimately, the land enjoyed forty years of peace as a result of Deborah's remarkable boldness and courage, and the people of God lived in freedom and without fear due to her mighty leadership.

Like Deborah, you are someone we can trust to help us overcome our obstacles and lead us to victory. Healthy Eights are empowering coaches and decisive problem-solvers. However, just as Deborah faced the risk of taking on too much responsibility as the ultimate decision-maker for all of Israel, it is crucial for you to avoid enabling the weak without first giving them the chance to cultivate their own strength. Drawing from Deborah's example with Barak, guide others to recognize their potential and provide them with opportunities to thrive, even if it means *not* taking charge when you are fully capable of doing so and allowing them to experience both success and failure.

The Good News for Defenders is that just as Barak wholeheartedly embraced Deborah, God fully embraces you. Whether in ancient times or the modern era, women often find themselves confined within culturally fabricated "feminine" boxes that demand warmth, softness, and submissiveness. However, not only did Barak accept Deborah as an authoritative representative of God, but he also invited her to join him in battle, embracing her commanding presence as a precious gift instead of feeling insecure about it.

In a world that frequently misunderstands the depth of an Eight's intensity, I encourage you never to apologize for who you are. Like Barak, we need to hear your voice, even if its words are tough to receive. God has lined up many spiritual victories, but sometimes the rest of us need that extra courage to confront our giants—which is why God gave us you.

→ Pray

Father, I am inspired by the example of Deborah, a compassionate and courageous leader. Help me to embrace my unique qualities without apology when people misunderstand my intensity, when I'm only trying to help. Use my strength, courage, and leadership to empower others to recognize and reach their highest potential.

Day 4 Reflections:

What is inspiring about Deborah's story? Which of her leadership qualities resonates deeply with you?

_____
_____
_____

How have societal expectations or misunderstandings affected your expression of intensity? How can you embrace your unique qualities without feeling the need to apologize?

_____
_____
_____

In which areas of your life may you be unintentionally preventing others from developing their own strength?

_____
_____
_____

→ Respond

Identify who the "Barak" is in your life and go and challenge them to take more initiative or responsibility. Don't let them continue to rely on you.

Day 5:

Flex Your Muscles

But be doers of the word, and not hearers only, deceiving yourselves.

—James 1:22

LOVE IS A VERB. OR AS RENOWNED author and speaker Bob Goff simply puts it: "Love does." Likewise, the apostle James calls us to be doers of the Word, rather than merely hearers, which aligns with your natural inclination to lead and *make things happen*. Your ability to swiftly transform knowledge into practical action showcases your remarkable superpower as a leader.

For all Defenders, actions speak louder than words. What a gift Eights are to the church, living in a world where people have become consumers of wisdom (often through books such as this) without ever letting their messages sink to the level of heart-actions. To borrow the apostle Paul's metaphor of the church being the body of Christ,

> I used to think being loved was the greatest thing to think about, but now I know love is never satisfied just thinking about it.
>
> –Bob Goff[7]

---

7   Bob Goff, *Love Does: Discover a Secretly Incredible Life in an Ordinary World* (Nashville, TN: Thomas Nelson, 2012), 17.

I see Eights as the muscular system, which grows in its ability to support the body through intense pushing, pulling, and the tearing-and-regrowing of muscle fibers. They push and pull an often lethargic church body through difficult conversations and experiences to help it work together to produce dynamic movement and culture-shifting strength. In other words, God uses Eights to "flex" and show the world what He's capable of.

Just as the apostle Paul exhorted his son in the faith, Timothy, to "fan" into flame "the gift of God,"[8] you too need to identify and honor the gifts you've been given so that you can set this world ablaze with the light and warmth of God's passionate love.

> For all Defenders, actions speak louder than words.

Eights are a leader's kind of leader, who are driven, capable, confident, fearless, and heroic. You have a big presence with an even bigger heart; when you walk into a room, the ambient temperature changes. You are direct, decisive, passionate, and resourceful, and your strong presence says, "I'm here to champion you and keep you safe."

Enneagram teacher Beatrice Chestnut, in her book *The 9 Types of Leadership: Mastering the Art of People in the 21st Century Workplace*, shares that Eights have the ability to see the "big picture," which allows them to see what needs to be accomplished and then get the right people in the right seats to get the job done. They carry a confidence that the rest of us envy, allowing them to overcome self-doubt and take on seemingly impossible tasks. Unaffected by a fear of failure or people's opinions, they'll do what's unpopular, make the difficult decision, or take bold action when change or justice is needed. Contrary to what often gets taught, Eights don't love conflict, but they *will* confidently walk into it in order to restore relationships and maintain forward motion.[9]

Eights strengthen others to do what they think can't be done and work for something larger than themselves, spotting mustard seeds of faith in every

---

8   2 Timothy 1:6 NIV

9   Beatrice Chestnut, *The 9 Types of Leadership: Mastering the Art of People in the 21st Century Workplace* (Post Hill Press, 2017), 258-259.

person and future possibility. Whether you are looking at a garage sale full of (what looks to everyone else like) junk, or showing up for someone who just got out of jail, you can take whatever raw material is available and build something great from the ground up. And when others start complaining that there is no money or resources to accomplish the vision, you say, "I'll find a way"—and you usually do.[10]

While it's true that Eight leaders often enjoy being in positions of prominence, they are also prepared to assume complete accountability for their actions and those of their followers and endure the repercussions of any failures.[11] Whereas unhealthy Sixes may blame others and unhealthy Threes jump ship at the earliest sign of failure, healthy Eights demonstrate a sense of commitment by taking ultimate responsibility for their team. They remain loyal, honorable, and supportive until the very end, even if it means going down with the ship.

The Good News for Defenders is that Jesus, with His sacrificial love, "took a bullet" for us by taking ultimate responsibility for our actions and suffered the consequences of our failures. Jesus didn't just talk about love but demonstrated it with action. To use the apostle John's words, "This is how we know what love is: Jesus Christ laid down his life for us. And we ought to lay down our lives for our brothers and sisters."[12]

→ Pray

Father, thank You for demonstrating love in action through the sacrificial love of Jesus, who took ultimate responsibility for my sins. Empower me to swiftly turn knowledge into action, being a doer of your Word. Equip me to flex my spiritual muscles and build up the body of Christ. Open my eyes wider to see all the potential in the world that You see.

---

10   Don Richard Riso and Russ Hudson, *The Wisdom of the Enneagram: The Complete Guide to Psychological and Spiritual Growth for the Nine Personality Types* (New York: Bantam Books, 1999), 308-309.
11   Riso and Hudson, *Personality Types*, 311-312.
12   1 John 3:16 NIV

Day 5 Reflections:

How does the concept of "love does" resonate with you as an Eight?

_____
_____
_____
_____

In what ways have you actively demonstrated love through your actions, rather than simply relying on words?

_____
_____
_____
_____

Identify and honor the unique gifts you possess. How can you maximize these gifts to set the world ablaze with God's love?

_____
_____
_____
_____

→ Respond

Write down a compelling vision for your family, team, church, or community that will mobilize them to take bold action, generate momentum, and work toward a larger purpose.

Day 6:

Jesus Is All In

For the eyes of the LORD range throughout the earth to strengthen those whose hearts are fully committed to him.

—2 Chronicles 16:9a NIV

IN A WORLD THAT OFTEN ENCOURAGES CAUTION and restraint, Defenders like you possess a unique strength: a willingness to be "all in," fully committed to whatever you set your heart on. Your intensity and determination set you apart.

Second Chronicles 16:9 reminds us that God's eyes roam throughout the earth, seeking hearts that are fully committed to Him. God, the Creator of the universe, sees you and values your unwavering dedication to what you believe in and your willingness to see it through.

> I suppose leadership at one time meant muscles; but today it means getting along with people.
> –Mahatma Gandhi[1]

Jesus, who quite literally went all in, endured opposition from sinful men but did not give

---

1 Chestnut, *The 9 Types of Leadership*, 251.

up.[2] He was direct, challenging others when they tried to manipulate Him;[3] He was assertive, not allowing anyone to control Him; and even though Jesus was harmed and killed, He pointed out, "No one takes [my life] from me, but I lay it down of my own accord."[4] While Jesus was with the disciples during His short ministry, He was their protector.[5] Most of all, He pursued justice and advocacy: "The Spirit of the Lord is upon me, because he has anointed me to proclaim good news to the poor. He has sent me to proclaim liberty to the captives and recovering of sight to the blind, to set at liberty those who are oppressed."[6]

While Jesus affirms the heart of an Eight, He also challenges any unhealthy version of what it looks like to be all in as a leader. No one would accuse Jesus of lacking in passion, yet He was patient with doubt—even from one of his closest followers, Thomas, who was skeptical about the resurrection and wanted more proof.[7] Like Jesus, you must "have mercy on those who doubt,"[8] and not interpret someone's initial resistance as an unwillingness to get on board.

> More power doesn't equal more influence.

But perhaps the greatest lesson Eights can learn from Jesus is that more power doesn't equal more influence. I know I told you yesterday to flex your muscles, but outright strength can easily become too much when you take the shortcut of simply bending your family, team, or community to your will. This autocratic instinct will get things done quickly at first, but it will ultimately decrease your impact as a leader.

True power is more than the ability to compel others to act according to your wishes, driving them where you will as though they were unthinking cars, idling motionless until directed by you. Rather, true power is strength under control,

---

2 Hebrews 12:3
3 Mark 10:18
4 John 10:18a
5 John 17:12
6 Luke 4:18
7 John 20:24-31
8 Jude 1:22

more like a horse than a vehicle. Horses have intelligence, strength, and speed but allow those qualities to be directed by a rider. You are called to have power, but it is not given to you to turn beloved members of the community into your machine; it has been given so that you might exert positive influence on the world, guided by the Rider.

Jesus had the influence He did by disarming the world instead of beating it. He was willing to "lose" to His enemies to inspire an even greater following. Though He had all authority on heaven and earth, He gives us the freedom to obey or disobey, to follow Him or walk away. His "inspire and align" over "command and control" strategy is what makes His leadership style so contagious. The next time you feel your gut telling you to push those around you harder, pause to ask whether this is a moment to patiently influence rather than forcibly drive.

The Good News for Defenders is Jesus will reward you for going all in. When the apostle Peter said, "We have left everything to follow you!" Jesus replied, "Truly, I say to you, there is no one who has left home or brothers or sisters or mother or father or children or fields for me and the gospel will fail to receive a hundred times as much in this present age."[9] The eyes of the Lord have gone throughout the earth and landed squarely on you: He sees your loyalty and commitment and your dogged determination, and He delights in filling you up with all His strength and might to leave a far greater impact than you could ever ask or imagine.[10]

→ Pray

Father, thank You for the strength and unwavering dedication You have given me as an Eight. Help me to surrender my desire for control, recognizing that true transformation comes through setting an example. Knowing You notice my determination is reassuring. Fill me with Your might today to lead with grace and humility.

---

9   Mark 10:28-30a NIV

10 Ephesians 3:20

Day 6 Reflections:

In what ways can you relate to Jesus as the perfect Eight, who endured opposition, challenged others, and refused to be controlled?

Consider the distinction between power and influence. How has relying solely on your power and imposing your will affected your impact as a leader?

How can you cultivate a more disarming and less aggressive approach in your interactions and leadership style?

→ Respond

Choose one specific project, relationship, or team where you want to focus on cultivating influence rather than relying solely on power. Write down what adjustments you want to make moving forward to inspire for maximum impact.

Day 7:

Clothed with Power

But you will receive power when the Holy Spirit has come upon you, and you will be my witnesses in Jerusalem and in all Judea and Samaria, and to the end of the earth.

—Acts 1:8

WORLDLY POWER IS EXERTED ON US EVERY day by individuals, government, corporations, and yes, religious institutions—all of whom seek to use, manipulate, or dominate us for their own ends. As a result of power grabs and abusive authorities across history and personal experiences, some people assume that all use of power is corrupt and should be avoided.

But that couldn't be further from the truth: power is a gift to be desired. Power is what began and sustains the world and God's church. Jesus—who was miraculously conceived, anointed, equipped, and raised to life by the power

> I am not interested in power for power's sake; but I am interested in power that is moral, that is right, and that is good.
>
> –Martin Luther King, Jr.[1]

---

1 Calhoun and Loughrige, *Spiritual Rhythms*, 19.

of the Holy Spirit—told His disciples, "But you will receive power when the Holy Spirit has come upon you."[2] When that prophecy came to fruition on the day of Pentecost, it was one of the largest displays of power ever witnessed in the Bible. The sound of a mighty rushing wind came from heaven; tongues of fire appeared to rest on the heads of the men and women who knew Jesus and were committed to following His teachings; and they began miraculously speaking these in different languages, making them look drunk to the bystanders.[3]

After this momentous event, the Greeks wanted to go back to business as usual, quoting their philosophers and talking about deep things rather than living them. But the apostle Paul did not bend to their will and start writing eloquent sermons or position papers; he chose to keep hammering the power of Christ's death and resurrection, reminding the (Greek) Corinthian church that "the kingdom of God does not consist in talk but in power."[4]

> **Defenders are attracted to and appreciate the gift of power.**

Defenders are attracted to and appreciate the gift of power. You know how to get it, how to use it, and who has the most of it when you walk into a room. While some contemporary leaders might view the pursuit of greater power as inappropriate or contrary to biblical principles due to its association with privilege, higher social status, or dominance over others, Jesus demonstrated no hesitation in using His power. With it He made the blind see, the lame walk, the storms cease, the sick well, the possessed free, and the dead to life.

Eights undoubtedly possess a remarkable amount of raw energy compared to other Enneagram types. You are like a clothes dryer plug, operating on a significantly higher voltage, while other types function more like standard outlets. The abundance of energy you receive from God allows you not only to drive significant change but also to accelerate the rate at which that change occurs. You are like a thermostat, quickly adjusting the temperature of the room,

---

2   Acts 1:8a

3   Acts 2:2-4

4   1 Corinthians 4:20

where other types are more like thermometers and can only read it. This is why you are a pacesetter and culture maker.

Though most teachers describe as Eights as "Challengers" because they can be aggressive, I chose to use the term "Defenders" instead, because the reason Eights challenge anyone is to protect either themselves or others. You are like a lightning rod, channeling God's good supernatural power and keeping the house from burning down when an unexpected strike hits. And when the storms of life come our way and take out our power, leaving us in the dark, you are like the generator we need to restore our well-being.

The Good News for Defenders is that we've been "clothed with power from on high"[5] to selflessly serve, not selfishly preserve. It's crucial to remind ourselves and others that the Holy Spirit has granted us far more power than we might realize—and in different forms. For example, Peter Scazzero, in his book *The Emotionally Healthy Leader*, highlights how positional power can be acquired through titles, roles, gifts, knowledge, and reputation.[6] Therefore, because this comes more naturally to you, encourage others to take stock of their power and start owning it!

Furthermore, it's essential to recognize that some individuals may have less cultural power due to factors like age, gender, ethnicity, or economic status. In such cases, we must emulate Jesus by working even harder to share whatever power we possess, empowering those around us and fostering a more equitable and just environment.

→ Pray

Father, I praise Your Son, Jesus, for being crucified in weakness so I would be able to live by the power of God with Him forever.[7] Help me to be a leader who encourages others not to shy away from the power they've been given but to steward it for the protection of others.

---

5 Luke 24:49

6 Peter Scazzero, *The Emotionally Healthy Leader: How Transforming Your Inner Life Will Deeply Transform Your Church, Team, and the World* (Grand Rapids, MI: Zondervan, 2015), 245-247.

7 2 Corinthians 13:4

Day 7 Reflections:

When have you used your raw energy to protect others or make a significant impact on driving change in your community or workplace?

Have others ever made you feel ashamed of your power or suppressed your urge to wield it? How did this impact you?

Who can you encourage today to recognize and own their power for positive transformation?

→ Respond

Lead a one-on-one or team meeting about owning your own power, asking questions such as: "What gifts, skills, and assets do you have? Who has given you permission to speak into their lives? What power do you have based on your age, ethnicity, gender, or other cultural factors? How can you give power away to those who have less?"[8]

---

8 Scazzero, *The Emotionally Healthy Leader*, 248.

Day 8:

Larger Than Life

Whoever is slow to anger is better than the mighty, and

he who rules his spirit than he who takes a city.

—Proverbs 16:32

UNAWARE OF THEIR SHEER STRENGTH, DEFENDERS ARE often likened to the proverbial "bull in a china shop." Author and Speaker Carey Nieuwhof shared that his former Director of Operations compared him to Bamm-Bamm on the old animated sitcom *The Flintstones*.[2] Bamm-Bamm was a toddler with superhuman strength who made audiences laugh with his excessive (and sometimes misused) energy.

> [An Eight's] larger-than-life energy doesn't fill a space; it owns it.
>
> –Ian Cron and Suzanne Stabile[1]

Healthy Eights are like a mighty dam built across a river, possessing an awe-inspiring reservoir of energy. They don't simply hold back or suppress their energy but channel it effectively to generate a steady and controlled

---

1 Cron and Stabile, *The Road Back to You*, 44.

2 Nieuwhof, Carey. "CNLP 241: Ian Morgan Cron on Using Your Enneagram Number to Boost Self-Awareness, Spiritual Growth and Reduce Conflict at Work and at Home." CareyNieuwhof.com, April 12, 2022. https://careynieuwhof.com/episode241/.

supply of power for countless people. In relationships, this ability to control the gates by making necessary adjustments to the flow of water makes their presence assertive yet approachable, slowing them down enough to make them consider how their actions and words affect others.

The wise sage of Proverbs says, "Whoever is slow to anger is better than the mighty, and he who rules his spirit than he who takes a city." In other words, the more commendable warrior relies on patience and self-control over brute physical strength and aggression. They learn just how much force is needed in each moment rather than discharging all their energy at once.[3] However, unhealthy Eights release the floodgates all at once, saying, "This is just how I am. Don't take it personally," often destroying relationships or even whole organizations in the process (such is their powerful potential). But healthy Eights will strive to understand how their big presence and big confidence may unintentionally intimidate family members, friends, or co-workers, and they will adjust their approach.

> [Healthy Eights] don't simply hold back or suppress their energy but channel it effectively.

I'm not suggesting you alter, hide, or suppress your authentic self. In Exodus 40:34, we learn that God's presence filled the Tent of Meeting, and its intensity was so great that it could be overwhelming for anyone who entered carelessly (and He was still holding back). It's essential to observe that God never expresses remorse for His formidable presence; instead, He directs His power wisely. My friend and Eight author Meredith Boggs explains, "Eights will never lose their passion, but they need to surrender their unbridled and untamed energy."[4] In other words, *power in moderation and power under control.*

Remember, the intensity of a bull elicits cheers in the ring, but not in a china shop. One hundred decibels is great for an action sequence in the movie theater but not for your small computer. The most expensive sound system can play our favorite music with crystal clarity and give us goosebumps, but that same music blasted through a small speaker will sound distorted and make us cover our

---

3 Proverbs 16:32
4 Boggs, *The Journey Home*, 42.

ears in agony. The reality is that most people don't have the "ears to hear" your preferred decibel level without you sounding garbled and "too much" to them. Thus, moderation is key while the rest of us upgrade our sound systems.

According to Beatrice Chestnut and Uranio Paes, some practical things you can do to implement this wisdom are paying attention to others' facial expressions or other forms of nonverbal communication, showing true remorse when someone tells you they feel hurt by you, and consciously training yourself to lower your energy level and smile more to help others feel more relaxed in your presence.[5] Approach others like a dry sponge, ready to absorb their emotions rather than wringing out all your passion on them. Work on taking up less space in the room, allowing others to feel comfortable occupying more for themselves—there's plenty to go around! Ask someone you truly trust today to give you direct feedback about how you are impacting others.

The Good News for Defenders is that self-control is a fruit of the Holy Spirit[6] and is available when you live *from* Christ's strength rather than your own. Surrender control to Him and draw on His strength, so you can cease striving to fill your perceived voids through sheer force of will. Don't worry: power under control and in moderation is not a pipe dream but a promise for all believers. When you learn to speak and live more dynamically—like a conductor guiding the music's rise and fall, rather than a radio on full blast—you'll quickly find that people will lean in, wanting more.

→ Pray

Father, help me to recognize and control my strength, applying it with wisdom and sensitivity. I surrender my unbridled energy to You and will embrace a balanced approach to life, relationships, and every situation I encounter. May my interactions be like a harmonious musical crescendo, drawing people closer and reflecting Your grace and love.

---

5 Chestnut and Paes, *The Enneagram Guide to Waking Up*, 218-219.
6 Galatians 5:22-23

Day 8 Reflections:

Reflect on a time when you unknowingly intimidated someone with your intensity. What were the consequences, and how did it impact your relationship?

Where does your intensity come from? Do you power up to overcome weakness, increase stimulation, avoid boredom, or use it as a substitute for expressing more vulnerable or tender emotions?

How would living from Christ's strength rather than for your strength lead to better results? How can you practice power in moderation?

> ### → Respond
>
> Authors Josh Green and Liz Carver recommend finding a place or practice where you can live at full volume. Find an outlet today where you can exert yourself fully without needing to "tone it down."[7]

---

7 Liz Carver and Josh Green, *What's Your Enneatype?: Understanding the Nine Personality Types for Personal Growth and Strengthened Relationships* (Beverly, MA: Fair Winds Press, an imprint of The Quarto Group, 2020), 149.

Day 9:

The Cursing Psalms

Be angry and do not sin.

—Ephesians 4:26a

A FRIEND RECENTLY TOLD ME, "I LOVE Jesus but I cuss a little." What do you think? Is loving Jesus and cussing antithetical? I once gave a sermon titled, "Should Christians Cuss, Drink, Smoke Marijuana, or Get a Tattoo?" because, as someone who wouldn't allow myself to cuss, I wanted to get to the bottom of whether or not it could be appropriate to drop a well-placed f-bomb or if God had commanded His children somewhere to only ever say "crapola."

> He who is not angry when there is just cause for anger is immoral.
>
> –Thomas Aquinas

I discovered that, while the Bible doesn't give us a list of cuss words, it does offer some helpful categories. For instance, taking the Lord's name in vain is always off-limits,[1] as are filthy or crude jokes that stem from an immature or discontent heart[2] and corrupt or destructive talk that

---

1 Exodus 20:7

2 Ephesians 5:4

tears others down instead of building them up.³ I shared with the members of our church that, after carefully considering all the biblical evidence, I believe there is space for a God-fearing and mature Christian to use a properly-placed word in the right context to express a seemingly inexpressible emotion.

Rather than judging others for using strong words on a list that doesn't exist or endless hand wringing about our own vocabulary, we should make space for those who want to use emotive language to call our attention to the pain, suffering, and evil in the world. In the New Testament, for example, Jesus referred to Peter, His right-hand man, as "Satan,"⁴ labeled the Pharisees as "snakes,"⁵ and denounced a proselyte of the Pharisees as a "child of hell."⁶ These instances exemplify the deliberate and purposeful use of strong language.

In the Old Testament, the imprecatory Psalms,⁷ which some call the cursing Psalms, provide an example of God creating space for us to pray in anger. Because Jesus tells us to love our neighbors and forgive our enemies, we *should* cringe when we read David's dehumanizing language about his enemies. Yet his words are *also*—at the same moment—accurate reflections of authentic human fear, anger, and pain and are an acceptable way to speak with God.

> **You have permission to be righteously angry.**

God didn't say anger is *never* allowed but rather, "Be angry and do not sin."⁸ Righteous anger is different from unrighteous anger in two important ways: first, righteous anger is *God-centered*—triggered by the same things that anger God, such as injustice and hypocrisy. Second, righteous anger is *controlled*—expressed in planned, often prophetic ways.

Righteous anger does not seek to destroy but is an expression of love meant to move us from the often unjust status quo, through disorientation, and into a new, more God-honoring order. We see throughout the Scriptures how righteous

---

3   Ephesians 4:29
4   Matthew 16:23
5   Matthew 23:33 NIV
6   Matthew 23:15
7   Includes Psalms 35, 59, 69, 79, 109, 137
8   Ephesians 4:26a

indignation leads to good action: God's anger toward sin moved Him to purify His people, and it led the prophets to take a stand in the face of injustice. In church history, we see leaders like Martin Luther break out in rage over abuses the church's leadership was carrying out against the people. His righteous anger toward practices within his own church, such as indulgences, sparked a worldwide reformation.

Like Luther, when Eights transmute their anger into good energy, they bravely pursue their divine calling and bring real change. As Riso and Hudson teach, "The actual energy of Eights is not anger or rage, although sometimes it can seem that way. Rather it is a passion and a total commitment to truth, life, and justice. It is a passion for the cause they believe in, or the people for whom they feel responsible."[9]

The Good News for Defenders is that you have permission to be righteously angry. Embrace the fire within and let your raw emotions rise to God like an overflowing river. Forget the fear of punishment; God wants to hear you out. Replace your polished requests with fervent cries. Be candid, knowing God can handle your cursing psalms. Release your anguish so that you can get to the bottom of your anger and discover your vulnerability and the true focus of your righteous angst. Then you will be held by God's loving arms and be able to channel your fire.

→ Pray

Father, though I sometimes despise the intense anger I feel, help me get in touch with my good anger and use it in a prophetic way. Help me pay attention to the impulses my body feels when I see sin and injustice around me. Give me the courage to express my anger authentically to You, trusting that You can receive it with understanding and love.

---

9 Rohr and Ebert, *The Enneagram*, 167.

Day 9 Reflections:

Do you think of your anger as an asset? Why or why not?

_____
_____
_____

What differentiates righteous anger from unrighteous anger? Can you recall a situation in your life where righteous anger led to positive change or action?

_____
_____
_____

Share about a time when you've openly expressed your raw emotions and felt a deeper connection with God. Consider how turning to God first in prayer can ease tension and improve your interactions with others.

_____
_____
_____

→ Respond

Read Psalm 109 and then write your own "angry" psalm to the Lord with the same level of intensity and vulnerability.

Day 10:

Strength and Swagger

But he said to me, "My grace is sufficient for you, for my power is made perfect in weakness." Therefore I will boast all the more gladly of my weaknesses, so that the power of Christ may rest upon me. For the sake of Christ, then, I am content with weaknesses, insults, hardships, persecutions, and calamities. For when I am weak, then I am strong.

—2 Corinthians 12:9-10

HAVE OTHERS SAID YOU HAVE A CERTAIN swagger about you? Don't deny it; you know it's true. Growing up, I lacked that self-confidence that comes so naturally to you, and fearing that I would finish last as the nice guy, I envied your confidence (and still do). One of the most famous swaggering characters in the Bible is Samson. While not the most healthy Eight I

> It's the paradox of the gospel:
> Strength is found in weakness.
> Control is found in dependency.
> Power is found in surrender.
>
> –Dan B. Allendar[1]

---

1 Dan B. Allender and Tremper Longman III, *Breaking the Idols of Your Heart: How to Navigate the Temptations of Life* (Downers Grove, IL: InterVarsity Press, 2007), 38.

know, we can learn a lot from his story.

Samson, possibly aligning with the One-to-One Eight subtype, was an incredibly powerful man, both in physical prowess and influence. He was overly-confident and frequently broke rules, bucked norms, acted recklessly, and endangered not only his life and those of his countrymen. The Israelites found him intimidating, but he ultimately became a hero.

As a young man, he demonstrated his extraordinary strength by tearing apart a lion with his bare hands. Later, he used his strength for vengeance, single-handedly defeating a thousand Philistines using only the jawbone of an ass as his weapon. After spending the night with a harlot in the Philistine city of Gaza, he faced an attack from his enemies, and to their surprise, the World's Strongest Man lifted the entire city gate on his shoulder and carried it to the top of a hill.[2]

Sadly, Samson's trusted wife Delilah was persuaded by her fellow Philistines (Israel's sworn enemy) to discover the secret of his supernatural strength so they might finally defeat him. After initially deceiving her and eluding the Philistines' attempts to overcome him, Samson eventually confided in Delilah that his power resided in his uncut hair. While he slept, the Philistines cut off his hair, causing him to lose his strength, and they gouged out his eyes and imprisoned him.

> **Redefine strength as a gift of divine power that emerges from human weakness.**

The lesson for Defenders in this epic story is the call to discern the difference between self-aggrandizing swagger and divinely-given strength. Swagger and self-importance were the sources of all of Samson's problems. His overconfidence alienated him from his own people, stirred up his enemies' wrath, and blinded him to Delilah's betrayal—the very thing he feared the most in life. Similarly, when unhealthy Eights carry too much swagger, they tend to make their family more guarded around them and inadvertently turn friends into foes, only increasing their chances of getting harmed or betrayed.

---

2   Judges 16:3

Strength and swagger is the Eight's strategy for overcoming their feelings of vulnerability—it's why they're often called "Challengers" by other Enneagram teachers. Eights judge themselves harshly when grief, feelings of inadequacy, or other painful emotions start to make them feel "soft." Therefore, the growth path for Eights is to allow God to redefine *strength* as a gift of divine power that emerges from human weakness to justly and strategically defend His people. The apostle Paul teaches us that when we embrace vulnerability, God's power rests on us in a magnificent and unforgettable way.[3]

For example, when Samson was physically weak and imprisoned, God allowed him to feel the full weight of his failure, and to learn humility and vulnerability—only then did God begin to fill him with divine power as his hair began to grow back. Then, one evening during a grand feast, Samson was brought to a great hall to entertain his enemies. Blind and shackled, having finally acknowledged where his true strength was found, he called on God for one final act of strength. He pushed the load-bearing pillars of the hall, causing the entire structure to collapse, killing himself and three thousand Philistines—more enemies than he had killed in his entire lifetime of fighting.[4]

The Good News for Defenders is that all of our spiritual enemies were crushed in one final act at the end of Jesus' human life. The story of Samson points us to the truly innocent Judge who withheld vengeance. Because Jesus became astoundingly vulnerable for us, we've been made strong. Christ dares you to follow His example and be courageous enough to be vulnerable, resisting the urge to cover up that which you think others will use against you. Take off your armor, remembering that when you feel weak, you couldn't look any stronger to those you've committed to defending.

→ Pray

Father, heal the fear underneath that causes me to be aggressive. Help me know You will protect me, even when the "Delilahs" in my life attempt to exploit my weakness. Give me the courage to be more vulnerable like Jesus, redefining strength as a gift of divine power that produces supernatural results, not as something I muster up.

---

[3] 2 Corinthians 12:9-10
[4] Judges 16:23-30

Day 10 Reflections:

What do you appreciate about your self-confidence, self-assurance, and good swagger?

Like Samson, reflect on a time when your over-confidence led to an undesirable outcome. What lessons did you learn from that experience?

How can you embrace your softer side instead of rejecting it? What steps can you take to practice vulnerability more openly within your family, church, and workplace?

→ Respond

Because you don't always need to be the strong one for everyone else, take the opportunity to confide in someone you trust and let them know how they can be a source of strength for you.

Day 11:

Taking Charge

And he said, "With what can we compare the kingdom of God, or what parable shall we use for it? It is like a grain of mustard seed, which, when sown on the ground, is the smallest of all the seeds on earth, yet when it is sown it grows up and becomes larger than all the garden plants and puts out large branches, so that the birds of the air can make nests in its shade."

—Mark 4:30-32

LIGHTS, CAMERA, ACTION! DON'T YOU LIKE THAT word: *action*? Defenders are our directors in life, telling us what props to make, what lines to memorize, and where to go. You also don't mind being the producer, head writer, and lead actor who insists on doing all their own dangerous stunts. Your first name is not a noun, but an action verb, and *Momentum* is your middle name.

> Waiting on the Lord is a confident, disciplined, expectant, active, and sometimes painful clinging to God.
>
> –John Ortberg[1]

---

1 John Ortberg, *If You Want to Walk on Water, You've Got to Get Out of the Boat* (Grand Rapids, MI: Zondervan Publishing House, 2001), 180.

Day 11

The focus of attention for Eights is taking charge. You probably have a rich history of effortlessly (or even accidentally) assuming leadership roles in your professional and personal life, even if you haven't always fully understood why. While you might not always feel the need to be in charge, there's something instinctual about your ability to recognize and fill a power vacuum when you see it.[2]

As assertive and ambitious leaders who are future-oriented, Eights often feel that the world is going way too slow and will push to make things happen. Similar to Newton's first law of motion, they tend to view the rest of us as objects at rest that need to be acted on by an outside force to get our butts moving! Do you often look at the people around you with a skeptical eye, wondering if they are giving their best?

Without Eights, the world may still be living in the Stone Age. Never known for taking small steps, they often attempt giant leaps for mankind. Behind every major advancement in the cultural spheres of business, government, media, church, arts and entertainment, education, or the social sector, there's often an Eight who has convinced or cajoled their followers to dream bigger.

> Eights can't receive God's protection when they take action prematurely.

That being said, Eights sometimes have a hard time taking their feet off the gas, which can lead to driving themselves and their people a long way down the wrong road. Throughout the Bible, we find examples of enthusiastic leaders who thought they were two steps ahead of God. Abraham tried to push God's timetable up to receive the promised son by sleeping with his maidservant. Moses struck the rock at Meribah in anger after God wasn't working fast enough to provide water. King Saul grew impatient waiting for Samuel to arrive and offer a sacrifice before going to war, and he decided to just do it himself. Stories like these are a reminder for Eights to try to catch themselves when they begin to perceive God as being indifferent to their situation and therefore push too hard and too fast.

---

2 Chestnut and Paes, *The Enneagram Guide to Waking Up*, 209.

From an early age, Eights often get results from taking charge, so they develop an overreliance on taking action. But putting too much trust in their bold and forceful style may cause them to miscalculate and go too far, especially in situations that call for a more nuanced and balanced approach.[3] Additionally, if you go too fast without getting the proper buy-in from your people, you risk eroding their trust or just plain burning them out, impacting future endeavors. All that to say, Eights can't receive God's protection when they take action prematurely. Movement doesn't equal achievement, and just because you *can* take action doesn't mean you *should*. Busy wheels spin, but true success means actually getting to your destination the right way.

The Good News for Defenders is that God produces remarkable results when you learn to trust the process and refrain from rushing ahead. Just as Jesus compared the kingdom of God to a tiny mustard seed that grows over time,[4] your journey might not always be flashy, but it will be effective. Like a skilled gardener who plants seeds and patiently waits, you can plant your mustard seed of faith and let God handle the outcome.

You can work harmoniously with the talented gardeners in your life, collaborating to plant, water, fertilize, and weed at the right pace for growth to take place. Embrace the psalmist's wisdom to "wait for the Lord,"[5] understanding that, just as rests are part of the music, waiting itself is a form of action. The next time you get impatient and are tempted to use force, remember that the outcome you are looking for cannot be achieved by your willfulness but by God's will.

→ Pray

Father, teach me to have patience and trust in Your process. Help me find balance in my actions and wait on Your timing. Remind me to collaborate with others and allow them to be my brakes, keeping me from rushing ahead. I surrender my need for control to You today and put my trust in Your guidance and wisdom.

---

3 Beatrice Chestnut, *The Complete Enneagram: 27 Paths to Greater Self-Knowledge* (Berkeley, CA: She Writes Press, 2013).

4 Mark 4:31-32

5 Psalm 27:14

Day 11 Reflections:

Reflect on a time when you saw God's faithfulness in a time of waiting. How did that experience strengthen your trust in the process?

Think about a time when you pushed too forcefully with powerful statements or excessive action. How could a more balanced and nuanced approach have yielded better results?

In which area of your life do you feel the need to take charge and control over the environment or outcome right now? How can you surrender your willfulness to God's will?

> ### → Respond
>
> Before making your next significant decision, seek input from trusted colleagues, friends, or mentors. Engage in discussions and gather different perspectives to gain a more comprehensive understanding of the situation.

Day 12:

The God Who Declares

Death and life are in the power of the tongue, and

those who love it will eat its fruits.

—Proverbs 18:21

It's no secret that Defenders are known for their blunt and brutally honest words. As you may have experienced, it is no fun being around an unaware, unhealthy Eight. They are quick to anger, full of demands, insensitive to people's feelings, intimidating with their big talk, and manipulative with their big promises. After shamelessly venting their anger, these Eights justify their actions by saying, "I was just telling the truth." While we certainly need more of the truth, as Sarajane Case says, "Honesty without kindness is brutality."[1]

> Words matter, and the right words matter most of all. In the end, they're all that remain of us.
>
> –John Birmingham

Unhealthy Eights cannot and will not acknowledge how their words set their relationships on fire. In his letter to the churches, the apostle James warns, "So also

---

[1] Sarajane Case, *The Honest Enneagram: Know Your Type, Own Your Challenges, Embrace Your Growth* (Kansas City, MO: Andrews McMeel Publishing, 2020), 200-201.

the tongue is a small member, yet it boasts of great things. How great a forest is set ablaze by such a small fire!"[2] Every Eight—healthy or otherwise—cannot remind themselves often enough of just how much power is in their tongue.

That being said, healthy Eights are incredibly misunderstood because of their communication style. Compared to everyone else, Eights have a more commanding presence with words, often employing a much more clipped, laconic style in their spoken and written communication.[3] Why say ten words when three will do? And don't forget the three exclamation marks at the end!!! This is why people sometimes think you are angry with them. They don't fully grasp that Eights are compelled by the truth, and that this isn't due to a lack of tact but their desperate drive to have all the facts, cut through the fluff, and resolve conflict faster. Because others don't understand this, Eights are often asked to "tone it down" and become more palatable so that the rest of us can become more comfortable—and even more so if that Eight is a woman!

> Keep serving as God's megaphone, fearlessly amplifying His declarations of justice and truth—even when it makes others a little uncomfortable.

You'll be encouraged to hear that Christian Enneagram teachers Jim Cofield and Richard Plass note that we are all made in the image of the "God who declares."[4] God makes His heart known and does not leave us second-guessing. It is precisely because God has disclosed Himself so candidly in the Scriptures that we can relate to Him and flourish under His wisdom. Don't miss this: as His image-bearer, you help all of us see what God is like when you boldly and authoritatively declare your needs, frustrations, and values. The way you communicate encourages all of us to pursue courageous transparency over insecure obscurity.

Yet the growth path for you will be twofold: first, to make the effort of better understanding others' very different communication styles so that you can get

---

2 James 3:5

3 The word "laconic" comes from the original name for the part of Greece, Laconia, in which the fearsome, warlike, and famously terse-spoken Spartans lived.

4 Find out more about their ministry here: https://crosspointministry.com/.

better results. Second, it will be to soften your language when appropriate. Don't lose your urgency or drive for moving toward truth, but maybe ask a friend to edit that email before you send it to your boss; or talk through your frustrations with a trusted Nine companion before unloading them on your team member. Try seasoning your words with a lot more affirmation—even if you think people shouldn't be rewarded for just doing their jobs. Be more patient with types who need more time to process or work up the courage to be direct with you, and use warm body language to get others to open up more.

The Good News for Defenders is that Proverbs says life, not just death, is found in the power of the tongue.[5]

While our words can be used to tear others down, hurt, and cause damage, they can also be used to breathe life, empower, and build others up.

I must confess that I regularly misjudged Eights for their candid tongue before becoming aware of the Enneagram. I often misinterpreted your *confidence* as cockiness and your *passion* as a personal attack. But now that I understand you better, and have repented for my assumptions, I find your words full of life. It's refreshing to me that you don't complain, make excuses, or gossip; that you let your yes actually mean yes, and your no mean no. Keep serving as God's megaphone, fearlessly amplifying His declarations of justice and truth—even when it makes others a little uncomfortable.

→ Pray

Father, thank You for the gift of communication and the power of words. Forgive me for being too blunt and causing pain at times. Help me understand the impact of my words on others and use my communication style for their good, never just to vindicate myself. Let my speech be seasoned with love, grace, and empathy, spreading life to all who hear.

---

5 Proverbs 18:21

Day 12 Reflections:

When have you been asked to "tone it down" to make others more comfortable? How did that impact you?

How does understanding that you are made in the image of the "God who declares" encourage or inspire you today?

What steps can you take to honor the communication preferences of others, becoming more effective and improving your relationships?

→ Respond

Say "I'm sorry" to someone you may have hurt with your words unintentionally. Don't believe for a second that it's weak to admit you were wrong and ask for forgiveness—that takes courage.

Day 13:

Tap the Brakes

But he would withdraw to desolate places and pray.

—Luke 5:16

RESTLESS AND EXHAUSTED, MY FRIEND AND CO-PASTOR Jamison barely noticed he was driving 10 over the speed limit and still accelerating. It had been a few difficult years: a global pandemic, nationwide turbulence, and local difficulties, not to mention all the normal pains of life and ministry, so our team heavily encouraged us both to take sabbaticals. On the first day of Jamison's two-month period of rest, he found himself speeding down the interstate when he heard God almost audibly ask him, "Jamison, where are you going so fast? You have nowhere to be!" At that moment, my friend pumped the brakes and replied, "I don't know, Lord!"

> You have made us for yourself, O Lord, and our heart is restless until it rests in you.
>
> –St. Augustine

Defenders are like racers, pushing themselves to the limits, pedal to the metal. Like Jamison, you are probably a pacesetter who uses your high-octane personality as fuel to help your people go further faster. And this is all good and well—just so long as you remember to tap the brakes occasionally. It ain't easy for Eights to let Jesus take the wheel when they need the adrenaline flooding their veins and the car firmly under *their* control.[1]

Just like Martha in the Bible, you may find it hard to slow down and prioritize stillness and presence over constant action. All it took was one glance at her sister, Mary, just sitting there at Jesus' feet, lazy and unhelpful, for Martha to start brooding. When she couldn't hold it in any longer, she burst out angrily: "Lord, do you not care that my sister has left me to serve alone? Tell her then to help me."[2] Imagine the scene—Martha bossing *Jesus* around. Even so, her Messiah replied with obvious tenderness, "Martha, Martha, you are anxious and troubled about many things, but one thing is necessary. Mary has chosen the good portion, which will not be taken away from her."[3]

Enneagram author Christian Wilcox encourages Eights to practice what she calls *slow mornings*. This is waking up an hour before you usually do to dedicate time to silence, solitude, and activities that connect you to God and your heart—whether it's yoga, running, listening to music, or journaling. Create an aesthetically pleasing and sensory-rich environment to make your space more inviting and less dull.[4] If you purposely carve out physical and temporal space to slow down your day before it's even begun, choosing what is better, your rested mind will protect your choice and it will not be taken from you.

> It takes a lot of courage to turn around and face the music.

Slowing down will also help you learn from the past. Because Eights get more revved up about what's ahead on the road and rarely look in the rearview mirror, they may be more likely to make the same mistakes again. And unfortunately, *denial* is a recurring theme for average to unhealthy Eights. It takes a lot of courage to turn around and face the music, confronting painful childhood memories and past romantic and work relationships. But in the end, creating

---

1 Moser, *The Enneagram of Discernment*, 177.

2 Luke 10:40b

3 Luke 10:41-42

4 Christina S. Wilcox, *Take Care of Your Type: An Enneagram Guide to Self-Care* (New York, NY: Tiller Press, 2021), 159-160.

space in the *present* to reflect on your *past* will lead you to wiser actions and a more fulfilling life in the *future*.

The Good News for Defenders is that your strongest, most capable, and influential self will emerge from slowing down, not speeding up. Watch the way Jesus withdraws to quiet places to pray in the Gospels.[5] These slow mornings centered Jesus, allowing Him a healthier tempo of life and ministry. Unhealthy Eights will eventually drive off a cliff when they drive fast and furious, never taking their feet off the gas—and sometimes they take others with them. Imagine if Martha's frustrations had changed Jesus' mind, and He ordered Mary back to her busy duties as hostess! Both friends would have lost time with the Savior, and He would have been diminished in their eyes. Choose what is better: Sit at His feet and surrender all of your urges for intensity and control.

→ Pray

Father, teach me to tap the brakes and release my grip for intensity and control. Like Martha, I often feel restless and troubled about many things, yet You remind me that one thing is necessary. Help me to experience the beauty of slowing down and the joy of knowing I need You more than You need me.

---

5 Luke 5:16

Day 13 Reflections:

Where are you moving too fast right now in your life? Where might you be taking on too much?

What can you do to prioritize peace over planning in your daily life? Are there any specific practices, activities, sensory elements, or aesthetic changes you can try? Explain.

As you look in the rearview mirror of your life, what patterns do you notice that can help you take wiser actions in the future?

→ Respond

Put a day of solitude on the calendar right now. On that day, plan to answer these questions: Where do I feel burdened? Where do I feel blessed? What do I feel God calling me to do? Where do I need to wait on God?

Day 14:
Confrontational Intimacy

And [Jesus] said to her, "Let the children be fed first, for it is not right to take the children's bread and throw it to the dogs." But she answered him, "Yes, Lord; yet even the dogs under the table eat the children's crumbs." And he said to her, "For this statement you may go your way; the demon has left your daughter."

—Mark 7:27-29

DAN STARED ME DOWN ACROSS THE TABLE and pushed his stack of chips to the middle. I was a college student on a summer mission trip with my campus ministry and our trip leader, Dan, usually positive and inspiring, was at that moment putting immense pressure on me at the poker table. I looked at my cards again, swallowed hard, and pushed my remaining chips toward him. "All in," I said. His eyes got big and a smile swept across his face as he laid down his *losing* hand. I had won. Again and again that summer, Dan shared this story, telling others that he intentionally "bullied" me through the game to see what I was made of.

> Wrestling with God is a sign of intimacy. You can't wrestle with someone you're far away from.
>
> –Jon Acuff

Some people might view what Dan did as unchristlike. But not to Defenders! Eights want you to stand up for yourself and go toe to toe with them: it's not an act of separation but how you earn their respect. They challenge others and expect others, especially those in their closest relationships, to challenge them back. Testing, competing, verbal sparring, and even roughhousing are all ways for them to get closer to someone and bring out the best in them. It's actually more awkward for an Eight to establish an emotional connection over coffee or in a church small group compared to doing something physical or active. In light of all this, Enneagram author Ian Cron advises all the other types, "Try not to take it personally. As strange as it sounds, what feels like intimidation to you feels like intimacy to an Eight."[1] For them, conflict is connection.

One of the foundational tales of the Hebrew people is Jacob's wrestling match with God at the Jabbok River. As darkness falls, an "Unknown Traveler" wrestles with Jacob as he lies near the water's edge, and there they struggle until the horizon begins to brighten. Suddenly, this Unknown Traveler (who we come to believe is actually God), "touched" Jacob's hip socket, leaving the bone wrenched out of joint. He had lost, yet in a surprising twist, the injured and cornered Jacob didn't fold but found the courage to engage. God said, "Let me go ...." But Jacob replied, "I will not let you go unless you bless me."[2] Finally, God complied and changed Jacob's name to *Israel,* which means "one who struggles with God."[3]

> God respects people who aren't afraid to "wrestle" with Him.

Another odd but similar story comes from the New Testament, when a Syrophoenician woman (phonetically: non-Jewish) met Jesus along the road and begged to heal her demon-possessed daughter. In what seems to be a test, Jesus coldly told this suffering mother that the children of Israel must be "fed" before the Gentile "dogs." Still cringeworthy two thousand years later, the woman refused to be submissively silent or walk away defeated, and instead challenged Jesus' words, saying, "Yes, Lord; yet even the dogs under the table eat the children's

---

1 Cron and Stabile, *The Road Back to You,* 46.

2 Genesis 32:26

3 Genesis 32:28

crumbs."[4] Then, to our utter surprise (and relief), Jesus smiled at the audacity of her faith and healed her daughter on the spot! Her forthrightness went against the norm of polite society and was truly exceptional considering her status as an ethnic outsider and her undermining of traditional gender expectations.

The rather unusual stories of Jacob and the Syrophoenician woman appear to illustrate that God respects people who aren't afraid to "wrestle" with Him. This truth changes everything. What if God didn't want us to be the nice guy or nice girl who prays using sanitized words? What if He wants us to negotiate with Him like Abraham, plead with Him like Moses, argue with Him like Martha, or wrestle with Him in prayer like David?

The Good News for Defenders is that God loves those who strive and struggle. He's not the unchallenging God that many people imagine in their heads. He wants us to grapple with Him as a way of cultivating greater intimacy and strengthening our faith. I want you to view "confrontational intimacy"[5] as something to embrace rather than reject. You are made in the image of the God who is a challenger—whose bond of love is intensified, not weakened, by bold prayers, fearless questions, and audacious faith. Like He did with Jacob, God's waiting to bless you today. Don't let go of God until you receive His blessing!

→ Pray

Father, thank You for the examples of Jacob and the Syrophoenician woman. In a world that may suppress my confrontational nature, give me the wisdom to find the balance between being true to myself and respecting cultural norms. May my bold prayers, fearless questions, and audacious faith draw me closer to You.

---

4   Mark 7:28

5   Rohr and Ebert, *The Enneagram*, 164.

Day 14 Reflections:

When has your challenging nature led to a more profound connection to God? How does this experience contrast with the idea of offering sanitized prayers or sitting in submissive silence?

_____

_____

_____

How does the story of Jacob and the Syrophoenician woman wrestling with God affirm your challenging nature? Is this side of you welcomed or discouraged by your family, friends, or church?

_____

_____

_____

Who would you like to challenge right now in order to stand up for yourself or advocate for someone else?

_____

_____

_____

→ Respond

Challenge your family, friends, team, or small group to go hiking, running, or another physical activity you enjoy, using this time to bond and have honest conversations about God.

Day 15:
Scalpel over Sledgehammer

Have nothing to do with foolish, ignorant controversies; you know that they breed quarrels. And the Lord's servant must not be quarrelsome but kind to everyone, able to teach, patiently enduring evil, correcting his opponents with gentleness.

—2 Timothy 2:23-25

THE NINETEENTH CENTURY PHILOSOPHER ARTHUR SCHOPENHAUER CAME up with a parable popularly known as "the Hedgehog's Dilemma," in which a group of porcupines seek to get close to one another so that they can share their body heat during a very cold winter. However, due to the thousands of sharp quills on their back, which very practically protect them from predators, they must keep a safe distance from their closest "friends" to avoid poking each other.

> **There is nothing stronger than true gentleness and nothing gentler than true strength.**
> –St. Francis de Sales[1]

---

1 Wagner, *Nine Lenses on the World*, 432-433.

They desperately want physical contact with one another but know one of them will inevitably get hurt.[2]

The Defender's dilemma is the same: they desire physical and emotional intimacy but are constantly at risk of unintentionally poking others with their quills. What they perceive as "playful" can come across as aggressive. It doesn't take much for an Eight's quills to poke someone unintentionally—especially if they don't have thick skin (which isn't your fault).

The growth path for an Eight is to learn how to engage without it always descending into outright disagreement or quarreling. This is a vital skill because being known as a contentious person can radically change the trajectory of their family and careers. The apostle Paul told his disciple Timothy that one of the requirements of spiritual leadership is to be kind, not quarrelsome; that the Lord's servant must avoid being foolishly controversial at all costs.[3]

An unhealthy Eight will quarrel to feel alive, seeking to stir up emotions when things feel dull or boring. They may start a fight with a loved one based on the smallest provocation, then bring out a litany of long-held grievances. They may shift the focus of the conversation from the *actual* topic to trivial matters or unrelated issues. More

> By honing your energy like a surgeon's scalpel, you can make a lasting mark on others that doesn't leave any scars.

interested in proving themselves right than seeking the truth, many Eights have admitted to realizing they are wrong midway through a conversation but finding themselves unable to admit it because that would make them feel and look weak.

However, a healthy Eight undergoing a positive transformation will recognize that while a good verbal skirmish might be cathartic for them, it can be overwhelming for others. *Their* primary objective in a constructive argument is not to win but to achieve understanding and resolution. To accomplish this, they must genuinely listen to different perspectives with an open mind, and when

---

2 Walter Veit. "The Hedgehog's Dilemma." Psychology Today, March 28, 2020. https://www.psychologytoday.com/us/blog/science-and-philosophy/202003/the-hedgehog-s-dilemma

3 2 Timothy 2:23-26

disagreements arise, they must intentionally look for points of agreement and common ground before addressing differences. The next time someone triggers you with a statement, silently count to 10 or take a break altogether. Though it's tempting to respond to outbursts, remember that a gentle response often defuses tensions faster, as emphasized in Proverbs.[4]

Finally, rather than relying on intimidation to get results, persuade others with a more winsome and intellectual approach using evidence, reason, and logic—and *empathy*. Pastor Tim Keller taught that the best way to change someone's heart is not by throwing dynamite at the rock to get a reaction, but patiently drilling a hole into their hearts and sliding the dynamite in, leading to a much more transformative explosion.

Perhaps the best piece of wisdom I can relay is to view constructive confrontation as "going hard on the issue, and soft on the person."[5] Much like a healthy immune system sending out antibodies to fight the infection without attacking the rest of the body, we must identify the *issue* rather than the person as the main threat. In the same way, Eights can raise awareness about an "infection" without destroying the person or the relationship in the process."[6]

The Good News for Defenders is that God is the Master Surgeon who doesn't come at us with a sledgehammer but a scalpel.[7] He very carefully removes our unhealthy attitudes and behaviors without causing harm to us! As a recipient of divine healing, consider approaching others in the same way, taking care not to cause unnecessary harm with force. Rather, strive for a surgical precision that focuses on understanding the nuances of each situation and person involved. Embracing this careful strategy doesn't mean diluting your God-given strength but rather refining it. By honing your energy like a surgeon's scalpel, you can make a lasting mark on others that doesn't leave any scars.

---

[4] Proverbs 15:1

[5] Henry Cloud, *9 Things You Simply Must Do* (Nashville, TN: Thomas Nelson, 2004), 153.

[6] Ibid., 160-161.

[7] Case, *The Honest Enneagram*, 198-199.

> **→ Pray**
>
> Father, help me find the right balance between intimacy and sensitivity. Lead me to engage in conversations with a focus on understanding and resolution, choosing gentle responses that foster unity. Just as You heal without causing harm, empower me to leave positive marks on others through thoughtful and compassionate communication.

Day 15 Reflections:

When did you feel a strong urge to use a "sledgehammer" approach but instead approached the situation with precision and care? What was the outcome?

Can you recall a time when a conversation took a quarrelsome turn? What factors contributed to this escalation and what can you learn from it?

What are some practical things you can do to adopt the scalpel principle of "going hard on the issue, and soft on the person" in your interactions?

> **→ Respond**
>
> Choose your battles. Not every issue requires a full-blown debate. Prioritize which topics are worth engaging in and which ones can be let go to maintain harmony.

Day 16:

Conflict Activators

And Moses lifted up his hand and struck the rock with his staff twice, and water came out abundantly, and the congregation drank, and their livestock. And the LORD said to Moses and Aaron, "Because you did not believe in me, to uphold me as holy in the eyes of the people of Israel, therefore you shall not bring this assembly into the land that I have given them."

—Numbers 20:11-12

WHAT MAKES YOU FEEL STRESSED OUT? FOR Defenders, some of the most commonly mentioned stressors are feeling controlled and manipulated or undermined and blindsided. Other stressors include being around people who chronically whine, gossip, beat around the bush, can't make a decision, get in your way, or (this is a big one in relationships) keep asking, "Are you angry?" It's also anxiety-inducing to observe others using their power to harm people or not take any action in the face of evident injustice.

> **No pressure, no diamonds.**
> –Thomas Carlyle[1]

---

1 Iam A. Freeman, *Seeds of Revolution: A Collection of Axioms, Passages and Proverbs, Volume 1* (Bloomington, IN: iUniverse, World Harvest, 2014), 74.

When these things happen, you may find yourself suddenly at the breaking point, ready to blow up in spectacularly public ways, becoming bossy and strident, and refusing to be appeased. More than once, the humble-but-stressed-out Moses seemed to throw up his hands, telling God he would rather die than deal with the unfaithful Israelites for another moment. While the tantrums often occurred in private, Moses' meltdowns took place before the entire nation—like the one at Meribah, when he struck the rock.[2]

When faced with these stressors, Eights have a tendency to stoically hide their emotional strain, preferring to handle their challenges privately, without revealing the full extent of their struggles. Suzanne Stabile notes that when female Eights hit a wall, they tend to slide down it, get a good cry in, and go to bed.[3] This downward spiritual spiral for Eights leads them to withdraw from relationships and take on excessive workloads while relying on anger to drive them forward. It's only when their health begins to deteriorate that they reluctantly acknowledge their stress.[4]

> Jesus was struck at the cross yet reverberated compassion.

When stress reaches a tipping point for Eights, they may move to the low or high side of Type 5 to cope. When healthy, this retreat involves introspection, solitary contemplation, and a meticulous gathering of information to discern the way forward. When unhealthy, this shift may take the form of overlooking self-care or compromising their sleep patterns and dietary habits. When Eights become withdrawn and detached, it often comes as a strange surprise to others who are used to their more outgoing, assertive selves.[5]

Here are some warning signs you can keep an eye out for that will assist you in recognizing when the check engine light is about to come on: enduring persistent bitterness, harboring paranoid thoughts of betrayal, desiring isolation, adopting

---

2 Numbers 20:10-13

3 Suzanne Stabile, *The Path Between Us: An Enneagram Journey to Healthy Relationships* (Downers Grove, IL: InterVarsity Press, 2018), 30-31.

4 Riso and Hudson, *The Wisdom of the Enneagram*, 300.

5 Ibid., 306.

the mindset of an outlaw with a license to break the rules, or quietly strategizing ways to retaliate against those you perceive as "enemies."

Reflecting on Moses' story, it's apparent he had a very stressful job—in the hot desert no less—and it's certainly understandable that he bent past the breaking point at times. He listened to constant complaining, bickering, and backsliding; his leadership and authority were under constant threat by his own friends and family. There's a good chance we too would have had a public meltdown. Perhaps you've already experienced something like this in your life or work and have suffered the consequences like Moses, whom God denied entrance to the Promised Land.

The Good News for Defenders is that there is a way to bend without breaking. Life and leadership situations may stress you, but the God who embodies "merciful and gracious, slow to anger and abounding in steadfast love and faithfulness"[6] will restore and fortify you.

God's patience is enduring; He waits calmly before displaying anger. His restraint prevents reactive behavior, showcasing mercy and forbearance. And just as Jesus was struck at the cross yet reverberated compassion in a remarkable demonstration of self-control, you too can pour out grace on even the most passive or controlling people in your life. God is willing to give you a longer fuse so you can act honorably before all and "uphold [God] as holy in the eyes of the people,"[7] and when those moments occur where you don't react the way you'd hoped, there is still time to repent and fulfill your work—like Moses, who faithfully brought his people to the doorstep of the Promised Land.

The next time you feel the kettle getting hot, don't isolate or hide. Turn to Christ and a trusted confidant. Permit them to address warning signs without downplaying their concerns.

---

6   Psalm 86:15b

7   Numbers 20:12b

> **→ Pray**
>
> Father, thank You for sending Your Son to be our example of someone who bent without breaking. Through temptation, opposition, persecution, and even death, He did not fold. Oh Lord, let the same compassion flow out of me that flowed out of Jesus when He was struck on the cross.

Day 16 Reflections:

When was the last time you subjected yourself to intense pressure? Did the results justify the exertion? How could you have shown yourself a little more leniency?

_____
_____
_____

What activates your stress most often? Are there common themes or triggers? Explain.

_____
_____
_____

How can you address your anger now to prevent a public meltdown like the one Moses experienced?

_____
_____
_____

> **→ Respond**
>
> Because others may be able to see the warning signs before you do, ask someone to share how they can tell when you are stressed out.

Day 17:
Nebuchadnezzar's Narcissism

While the words were still in the king's mouth, there fell a voice from heaven, "O King Nebuchadnezzar, to you it is spoken: The kingdom has departed from you, and you shall be driven from among men, and your dwelling shall be with the beasts of the field. And you shall be made to eat grass like an ox, and seven periods of time shall pass over you, until you know that the Most High rules the kingdom of men and gives it to whom he will."

—Daniel 4:31-32

IN ONE OF THE WILDER STORIES FROM Scripture, the legendary Nebuchadnezzar ruled his ascendant Babylonian Empire with an iron fist. He had it all: power, prestige, and a big personality. From his impressive seat in the heart of the Fertile Crescent, he looked upon his grand city and the empire it represented, and he loudly proclaimed just how amazing he was to have accomplished all of that greatness *all on his own*.

Soon after this episode, Nebuchadnezzar experienced disturbing dreams and

> Nearly all men can stand adversity, but if you want to test a man's character, give him power.
> –Abraham Lincoln

sought the counsel of Daniel, a wise young captive from Israel, a nation recently conquered by the king. After interpreting the dreams through divine insight, Daniel warned the king about the consequences of his unchecked pride and the impending downfall if he didn't change his ways. Despite the warning, Nebuchadnezzar's arrogance persisted, leading to a harsh reality check that humbled him drastically. Once a mighty ruler, he was reduced to a solitary existence in the wilderness, where he recognized his limitations and gained a newfound perspective. Eventually, he was transformed, acknowledged his dependence on God, and offered credit where it was deserved.

Nebuchadnezzar's story is a reminder that some life lessons can only be learned the hard way. Defenders, by nature, often have to graduate from the School of Hard Knocks before advancing in life. Without a few humbling moments, this type can easily come to express classic traits of narcissism (as it's popularly understood). But let's get one thing straight: Narcissism can show up in every type. Though a character like Nebuchadnezzar may be viewed as your stereotypical Narcissist, the Bible is also full of "covert narcissists" who tend to be more subtle and focus on gaining control through manipulation or playing the victim. It is noteworthy that such covert narcissists can potentially cause even greater harm because they operate without arousing suspicion while garnering support from outsiders. This insidious behavior can result in significant emotional and psychological damage inflicted on those in close proximity to them that spans over an extended period of time.

> **Nebuchadnezzar pursued a superhuman status while Jesus willingly embraced His servanthood.**

Even the most self-assured leaders, such as Nebuchadnezzar, can experience moments of insecurity. They may feel compelled to compensate for any perceived weaknesses by projecting an image of strength, control, and power. To maintain their facade of invincibility, they often tell themselves: "I am stronger than others. No one can tell me what to do. I don't have to play by the rules." But here's the twist—these thoughts, while they may pump you up, become a self-protective shell that is nearly impossible to crack.

Enneagram authors Liz Carver and Josh Green describe the the growth process for Eights as "tenderizing." Just as meat becomes tender through repeated, forceful hits, an Eight's tough exterior can require consistent, significant force to break through and reach their true selves hidden behind their two-ton shield.[1] As we see in Nebuchadnezzar's story, it took a powerful blow to his pride for him to regain his place.

If you desire to become a more tender leader, you can choose the easy way or the hard way: taking gradual, conscious steps toward the goal of empathic love and understanding, or undergoing a tumultuous tenderization process. The path to transformation runs through both great love and great suffering. The former path is much less painful but still requires radical vulnerability through humbly sharing your weaknesses, trusting people who may let you down, handing over control to fallible people, or letting someone "less deserving" take the credit.[2]

The Good News for Defenders is that Jesus has shown us the way into this path of *downward mobility* out of narcissism. As Paul sings in his letter to the Philippians, Jesus "did not count equality with God a thing to be grasped, but emptied himself, by taking the form of a servant."[3] Nebuchadnezzar pursued a *super*human status while Jesus willingly embraced His servanthood by fully identifying with humility. Just as our Messiah condescended from His seat of glory, voluntarily taking on human flesh with all its limitations and vulnerabilities, have that same mindset today by allowing yourself to decrease so that others may increase.

→ Pray

Father, thank You for Your Son Jesus, who took the form of a servant rather than grasping for the power that was rightfully His. Help me discern the balance between self-assurance and humility, understanding that my strength is a gift from You to use for others. Give me the strength to humbly embrace my weaknesses and become a tender leader.

---

1 Carver and Green, *What's Your Enneatype?*, 149.

2 Ibid., 149.

3 Philippians 2:6-7

Day 17 Reflections:

When did you experience a humbling moment like Nebuchadnezzar? How did this experience change you?

Where might there still be areas of unchecked pride in your life?

Compare Nebuchadnezzar's journey with Jesus' example of humility. How does Jesus' humble nature inspire you to cultivate a more selfless and servant-hearted approach to life?

→ Respond

Identify a situation where you can practice letting someone else take the lead.

Day 18:

Thriving at Work

Then I said to them, "You see the trouble we are in, how Jerusalem lies in ruins with its gates burned. Come, let us build the wall of Jerusalem, that we may no longer suffer derision."

—Nehemiah 2:17

DEFENDERS ARE "BOSSES" WHO TYPICALLY RISE TO the top of an organization faster than anyone else because of their inherent drive, natural leadership abilities, and willingness to step up to the plate when others are too passive or afraid. All Eights are "activators": people who refuse to merely "pray about it," instead living by the motto, "Just do it!"

> God isn't offended by your biggest dreams or boldest prayers. He is offended by anything less.
>
> –Mark Batterson[1]

One such biblical character was the fifth century BC Jewish deportee, Nehemiah, who supervised the rebuilding of Jerusalem. After hearing his beloved Jerusalem's walls were broken down and its gates destroyed by fire, he sat and wept for days—praying and

---

1 Mark Batterson, *The Circle Maker: Praying Circles Around Your Biggest Dreams and Greatest Fears* (Grand Rapids, MI: Zondervan, 2016), 15.

fasting. But rather than sending his thoughts and prayers and waiting for God to send someone else, he stepped up. With the Babylonian Emperor's approval, Nehemiah traveled to Jerusalem, secretly surveyed the rubble, and determined the size and scope of the project. Then, to everyone's surprise, this cupbearer received permission to rebuild the city originally destroyed by Babylon from its king, Artaxerxes. Not only that, but he got the king to donate all the supplies for the massive project and provide a military escort![2] As if getting the project off the ground was not difficult enough, once the rebuilding work began, the Jews' neighboring enemies plotted to come in and halt their progress, so Nehemiah told his workers to carry a hammer in one hand and a weapon in the other.[3]

Similar to Nehemiah, Eights display decisive leadership that gets people in the right seats and empowers them to drive forward with full force. They have the confidence to take on tough challenges,

> Eights display decisive leadership that gets people in the right seats.

make big requests, acquire resources, and offer protection. In the workplace, working alongside healthy Eights is incredibly energizing and confidence-boosting, because they lead with passion, have your back, put a lot of energy and effort into what they do, aren't afraid of constructive conflict, and strive to see you succeed. When the team gets stuck in endless discussions, an Eight can cut through to the point and help them make a decision. While others gossip, the Eight stays direct and honest, letting everyone know where they stand. Eights prefer mentoring over micromanaging, giving others the opportunities to either succeed and grow or fail and learn.[4]

When they aren't the boss, though, Eights need a few things in order to thrive: autonomy and control over their work and process, real challenges that require strategic thinking and overcoming obstacles, direct communication, a result-oriented culture, room to advance in the organization, and respect. Younger Eights may need to stay busy with multiple projects, or they can cause trouble. As Cron and Stabile share, "A bored Eight is like a puppy who's been cooped up

---

2 Nehemiah 1:3–2:8
3 Nehemiah 4:17
4 Chestnut, *The 9 Types of Leadership*, 266-269.

in the house all day: keep him busy or he'll gnaw everything in your house down to the studs."[5]

While Eights have many impressive strengths, their "all or nothing" mentality makes it hard to know when to stop. Average to unhealthy Eights tend to overextend themselves to the point of exhaustion, charging ahead without listening to others' points of view, dismissing relevant details, and getting very impatient with excessive planning or indecision. The key for them to remain an *asset* and not turn into an *ass* (I'm not talking about you though) is to be aware of their desire to push ahead and purposefully work against it, allowing things to happen rather than forcing the issue.

The Good News for Defenders is though Nehemiah felt powerless working in the king's court, God opened a door to a new challenge that would end up influencing the Jewish nation forever. Because Nehemiah didn't just "pray about it" but also got to work, he paved the way for the Messiah's triumphal entry into Jerusalem. Like Nehemiah, God will use you to do things that seem impossible and have an effect that can reverberate across generations. But you must not act too quickly; slow down to pray and fast like Nehemiah first, and allow yourself to attend to details and even second guesses. Then and only then will you be able to build something that will last and be able to look back and say "for the good hand of my God was upon me."[6]

→ Pray

Father, thank You for giving me incredible gifts and abilities. Like Nehemiah, I know that if I ask anything in Your name You'll make it happen in Your way and in Your time.[7] Help me to keep praying big, bold prayers as I dream about what could be. Slow me down enough today to listen to Your voice. I know if I acknowledge You first, my paths will be straight.[8]

---

[5] Cron and Stabile, *The Road Back to You*, 56.
[6] Nehemiah 2:8b
[7] John 16:23
[8] Proverbs 3:5-6

Day 18 Reflections:

Which of the workplace strengths do you see most in yourself? Please explain.

What do you need in your workplace to thrive? Have you communicated these to your boss or team?

What can you do to slow down and create a better work-life balance?

→ Respond

Write down a seemingly impossible project you would like your team to accomplish if you knew God's hand was on you. Then rally the troops to pray, fast, and run after it.

Day 19:
Authority over Anarchy

And Jesus came and said to them, "All authority in heaven and on earth has been given to me. Go therefore and make disciples of all nations, baptizing them in the name of the Father and of the Son and of the Holy Spirit, teaching them to observe all that I have commanded you. And behold, I am with you always, to the end of the age."

—Matthew 28:18-20

IMAGINE DRIVING TO WORK TOMORROW, ONLY TO find that every traffic signal has vanished. Not only that, but everyone seems to have forgotten the basic rules from Driver's Ed. Streets once bustling with order now echo with honking horns and screeching brakes while pedestrians risk their lives crossing chaotic intersections. That's what anarchy looks like—no clear rules, norms, or expectations, only chaos. But authority brings order and safety and keeps the traffic flowing so you can get where you want to go.

> Introduce a little anarchy. Upset the established order, and everything becomes chaos.
>
> –The Joker[1]

---

1 "Joker's Quotes." IMDb. Accessed November 9, 2023. https://m.imdb.com/list/ls066080076/mediaviewer/rm2032441344?ref_=img_list_media.

However, due to the constant misuse of authority from leaders in nearly every capacity, some have tried to overcorrect by resisting all forms of established order. While flattening the hierarchy sounds good in theory, it doesn't necessarily solve issues related to conflicts, accountability, efficiency, and other challenges. That's why, as Jesus was preparing to pass the leadership baton to His disciples, He said, "All authority in heaven and on earth has been given to me. Go therefore and make disciples of all nations."[2] He knew exponential multiplication would require the use of delegated authority.

Defenders have a closer relationship to authority than any other type (for better *and*, at times, for worse). When healthy, Eights use their authority to cast vision, rule with justice, remove dead weight, establish clear lanes, and create a culture of honor and accountability. They can make the decisions no one else wants to make because respect is more important than approval.

Like Jesus' disciples, you must learn to live under authority before exercising healthy authority. This entails first acknowledging, rather than invalidating, authority figures above you. Unhealthy Eights often demand submission to their authority while living as unsubmissive rebels, evading accountability. When not in power, Eights tend to consistently challenge and test authority. My nine-year-old son, for example, is a classic Eight. He tests me relentlessly, staring into my eyes with the same intensity as a grown adult, daring me to tell him *no*.

> The big idea is responsible dominion, not dominance.

My other son is a twelve-year-old Counterphobic Six (a subtype that outwardly resembles an Eight). When he found some of his middle school teachers to be unfair in their posture toward him, he wanted to rebel. For him, if authorities can't be trusted to take right action, why obey them? In situations like these, it can be very difficult to comply, but our command from Paul is clear, in that we are to be "subject to the governing authorities."[3] However, I must stress that when true injustice is identified, that submission is no longer a given. It is then we need the Defenders in our lives to stand up and lead us into justice.

---

2   Matthew 28:18-19

3   Romans 13:1

The Good News for Defenders is that authority is not a curse but a gift from God. Going all the way back to Genesis, God commanded Adam and Eve to take dominion over the earth's resources and inhabitants. The call is the same for you today—show the world what God is like by taking ownership over the natural world to make earth more like heaven, not with reckless exploitation but loving benevolence. The big idea is *responsible dominion,* not *dominance.*

Healthy Eights exercise dominion in their spheres of influence by offering more *care* than *control.* Because the average Eight doesn't always feel the need to be close friends with coworkers, reaching out to make more meaningful social connections and offering care and concern can build trust.[4] Sharing more personal stories from your life and offering more of your tender side will add a lot of relational capital and help moderate the unintentional intimidation factor. This can lead to the sort of relationships where you can receive constructive feedback from trusted peers.

If you want God to trust you with more authority, the most important thing you can do is find somebody you're willing to submit to. Pastor AJ Sherrill says *accountability* must be one of your primary spiritual disciplines. Inviting feedback from trusted friends must be intentionally sought, or it probably won't happen.[5] Find those who can speak truth into your life and give them the freedom to speak.

→ Pray

Father, I want to lead well and honorably. Give me the capacity to connect with and care for those under my authority. Help me submit to all imperfect, earthly authorities, reminding me that submitting isn't always losing. Direct me to trustworthy people in my life who can guide me and hold me accountable.

---

4   Stabile, *The Path Between Us,* 31.

5   AJ Sherrill, *The Enneagram for Spiritual Formation: How Knowing Ourselves Can Make Us More Like Jesus* (Grand Rapids, MI: Brazos Press, a division of Baker Publishing Group, 2020), 78.

Day 19 Reflections:

How have you witnessed others trying to "flatten the hierarchy"? How did this approach fall short in addressing conflicts, accountability, bottlenecks, or other challenges?

_____
_____
_____
_____

When have you struggled with submitting to authority figures? What have you learned from those experiences?

_____
_____
_____
_____

What will you do to add more tenderness, love, and care to your authority?

_____
_____
_____
_____

→ Respond

Ask someone to call you out when you need it. Having someone who can tell you when you're being too blunt or forceful will only make you more respectable to everyone. So, who will you ask today?[6]

---

[6] Kim Eddy, *Enneagram for Beginners: A Christian Guide to Understanding Your Type for a God-Centered Life* (New York, NY: Penguin Random House LLC, 2020), 146.

Day 20:

Lust for Intensity

Be still, and know that I am God. I will be exalted among the nations, I will be exalted in the earth!

—Psalm 46:10

I'M NOT A HANDYMAN, BUT I PRETEND to be when I'm holding a power tool. Even after watching multiple DIY videos, it's almost guaranteed that I'll mess up whatever project I'm working on. On more than one occasion, zeal for my power drill resulted in an over-tightened screw, stripped bare, leaving nothing to work with. Defenders are like power tools compared to the rest of us, who come at life's problems holding our little screwdrivers—but your innate power can sometimes go a little too far without the right touch.

> We need to find God, and He cannot be found in noise and restlessness. God is the friend of silence.
> –Mother Teresa[1]

The vice, or deadly sin of an Eight, is *lust*. Much more than sexual interest, the Eight's Achilles' heel is a *lust for intensity* in all of life. While this starts out as an innocent desire to squeeze the most out of every moment, an Eight can quickly feel

---

1 Gordon MacDonald, *Ordering Your Private World* (Nashville, TN: Thomas Nelson, 2017), 129.

an excessive and urgent need to overdo everything—overindulge, over-work, overparty, overexcercise, overspend, or overreact.[2]

When an Eight gets swept up and carried away by the vice of lust, you may find yourself getting into power disputes, rebelling against or provoking others, communicating with too much forceful language, engaging in shock value storytelling, or saying things like "If you can't stand the heat, get out of the kitchen!" Make no mistake: We don't just see you as a power tool, but a power plant—and we thrive off of your thermal energy. Without you, we'd be sitting in the dark. But, just as a power plant needs control rods and cooling systems, so too does an Eight need to harness their lust to prevent a nuclear reaction.

For Eights to keep their pressure gauges balanced, remember that *bigger is not always better*, and that *less is more*. As a former pastor, it was very tempting to apply pressure to our team or work overtime to get more attendees on a Sunday morning. Numbers are not negative and can be a metric of success, but they can easily become a snare.[3] There seems to be a constant theme throughout Scripture that demonstrates God gets more glory when He gives us less to work with, not more.[4]

> Remember that bigger is not always better and that less is more.

Furthermore, God places boundaries around an Eight's passion for intensity to enhance pleasure, not diminish it. This truth is counterintuitive, but as Pastor Ben Patterson points out, the Colorado River is made more powerful by the limiting walls of the Grand Canyon: "Wider boundaries diminish the river; sharper, stronger, and narrower boundaries strengthen it. Less is more."[5]

Learn to limit yourself to the present rather than spreading yourself too thin. The grass is not greener on the other side, but wherever you water it. If you think that the kingdom is "out there," something to go after and conquer, rather than

---

2   Cron and Stabile, *The Road Back to You*, 45.

3   As was the case for King David in 1 Chronicles 21 when he commissioned Joab to conduct a census, putting his trust in his large army rather than God.

4   For example, in Judges 6-7, God intentionally dwindles down the number of Gideon's soldiers to prevent them from boasting in their own strength.

5   "The Goodness of Sex and the Glory of God," Desiring God, September 25, 2004, https://www.desiringgod.org/messages/the-goodness-of-sex-and-the-glory-of-god.

a sanctuary within your own soul, you'll be missing out.[6] Lust uncontrolled will cause you to fill the emptiness within by running after wild ideas and future possibilities, all the while missing the feast right before your eyes.

The Good News for Defenders is you won't find emptiness but God's presence in stillness. As the psalmist writes, "Be still, and know that I am God."[7] Elijah learned this firsthand. After the intense showdown between the God of Israel and the prophets of Baal on Mount Carmel (an Eight's dream of righteous confrontation), the prophet fled into the wilderness, wanting to die when the spectacular revival he expected didn't come. At Mount Horeb, however, God famously spoke to Elijah—not in the powerful fashion of fire, wind, or earthquake—but in a gentle whisper.[8]

Let this be a reminder that if you get off the treadmill of intensity and instead find contentment in the stillness of the present, you get to hear the gentle whisper of God speaking directly to your heart. Right now, quiet your racing mind, be still, and embrace silence—not as an enemy but as an invitation for God's voice to come and fill every void. The world won't stop spinning if you take some time to rest and recharge.

→ Pray

Father, squeezing every drop out of life can be invigorating, but I also acknowledge that it can lead me to overdo things, to indulge excessively, and to miss the beauty in simpler moments. Remind me that You don't just show up in fire, wind, or earthquakes but in stillness. Remind me that I don't need intense experiences to feel alive or in control.

---

6   Boggs, *The Journey Home*, 43.

7   Psalm 46:10

8   1 Kings 18–19

Day 20 Reflections:

Can you connect with the concept of "lust" as a need for intensity? Have you observed any areas where your pursuit of "bigger is better" has crossed into excess? Explain.

How can you embrace a "less is more" strategy and practice moderation by putting limits around your consumptions, expectations, or ambitions?

Instead of impulsively seeking intensity, how can you integrate more moments of stillness to ground yourself in the present and hear God's voice?

> ### → Respond
>
> Find a healthy outlet through a physical activity, creative pursuit, or leadership role that allows you to fulfill your need for intensity in positive ways.

Day 21:
Love Has a Backbone

I hate, I despise your feasts, and I take no delight in your solemn assemblies. Even though you offer me your burnt offerings and grain offerings, I will not accept them; and the peace offerings of your fattened animals, I will not look upon them. Take away from me the noise of your songs; to the melody of your harps I will not listen. But let justice roll down like waters, and righteousness like an ever-flowing stream.

—Amos 5:21-24

HATE IS OFTEN THOUGHT OF AS A strong word in the church. Yet, we can't deny that Proverbs rather bluntly says, "There are six things that the Lord *hates.*"[2] And the book of Amos shows God rebuking the people for their religiosity without substance—singing popular worship songs while grave injustices happened all around them. He said, "I hate, I despise your feasts."

> Injustice anywhere is a threat to justice everywhere.
> –Martin Luther King Jr.[1]

To truly love God, we must learn to love what He loves and *hate* what He hates—*injustice*

---

1 Martin Luther King, *Letter from the Birmingham Jail* (San Francisco: Harper San Francisco, 1994).

2 Proverbs 6:16, emphasis added

included. As Pastor Bryan Loritts aptly states, "Love has a backbone."³ Eights, whom I previously likened to the muscles of the body of Christ on Day 5, are more accurately the entire musculoskeletal system, encompassing even our bones. In essence, Eights serve as the church's backbone, providing robust support and fostering unwavering confidence.

Just as the skull shields the brain and the rib cage safeguards the heart, Eights stand as protectors of the world's most vulnerable parts—the frail, exploited, and disadvantaged. Possessing the largest capacity for creating justice, they vehemently oppose any exploitation of those with less power. They don't merely observe injustices but respond urgently, driven by their righteous indignation.

I'm sure this doesn't come as a surprise, but it's evident that the church has frequently lost its backbone. Nowadays, the church more often resembles a jellyfish than the *ichthus*-fish symbol used by early Christians, who regularly faced persecution and spoke up against the injustices of the Roman Empire. Jellyfish-like Christians tend to shy away from confrontation or threats, prioritize surface-level harmony over addressing critical issues, and prefer going with the flow rather than against it. They fear saying the wrong things or appearing too radical in the eyes of others, worrying about potential harm to their reputation or church attendance.

> To truly love God, we must learn to love what He loves and hate what He hates.

This problem of peace*faking* as opposed to peace*making* goes all the way back to the Old Testament when the prophet Jeremiah, in Eight-like fashion, brought his megaphone to the assembly to call out the spineless clergymen for proclaiming, "'Peace, peace,' when there is no peace."⁴ Even our most well-intentioned efforts fall short if we don't take action and hold people accountable. True peacemaking is not simply doing our best to "talk it out" and seek compromise; it's also intervention—challenging others to take ownership of destructive or harmful behaviors and set a course of action that leads to restoration and restitution. *That's* Biblical justice.

---

3   Bryan Loritts, *Insider Outsider: My Journey as a Stranger in White Evangelicalism and My Hope for Us All* (Grand Rapids, MI: Zondervan, 2018), 171.

4   Jeremiah 6:14

Your unique role as a Defender is to firm up any flabbiness you see in the church's justice efforts, to empower those around you to confront injustice, take a stronger stance on helping the poor and marginalized, and fortify a commitment to diversity and equity. Though this work is not on you alone, you can create a justice ecosystem right where you are at by launching special events, mentoring groups, cohorts, book studies, community partnerships, or educational workshops to get some momentum going. These efforts often take years to get the flywheel moving, but once it does, you'll have an army of allies, advocates, and activists.

The Good News for Defenders is God is "the Rock, his work is perfect, for all his ways are justice."[5] As one who has been given the torch to "let justice roll down like waters, and righteousness like an ever-flowing stream,"[6] don't stop running. I see you putting yourself in jeopardy for the sake of justice and fairness for all. I see you identify with the oppressed and respond swiftly when others are violated, feeling as though you yourself have been violated. You demonstrate with your actions that true love does not tolerate injustice when it is supported by the backbone of truth.

→ Pray

Father, I praise You for being my Rock and Refuge. Just as You rebuked those who remained passive amid injustice, give me the courage to stand up boldly against it. And because it can be tiring, give me more of your supernatural strength and determination to champion Your causes, even when the church appears complacent.

---

5 Deuteronomy 32:4

6 Amos 5:24

Day 21 Reflections:

How does the concept of you being a "backbone" align with your sense of purpose and role within your faith community?

_____
_____
_____
_____

When have you harnessed your strength to confront injustice and align with what God hates?

_____
_____
_____
_____

What is the next best thing you can do to continue building a justice ecosystem of allies, advocates, and activists within your context?

_____
_____
_____
_____

→ Respond

Identify areas of complacency within your church or workplace that need to be addressed. Think about specific actions you can take to challenge and change these situations.

Day 22:

Blind Spots in Love

Love is patient and kind; love does not envy or boast; it is not arrogant or rude. It does not insist on its own way; it is not irritable or resentful; it does not rejoice at wrongdoing, but rejoices with the truth. Love bears all things, believes all things, hopes all things, endures all things.

—1 Corinthians 13:4-7

IT TAKES A WHILE FOR DEFENDERS TO trust someone, but once they do, they're *all in*. Defenders in love are devoted life-long partners who don't leave when the relationship gets hard. Their passion and protectiveness are a tower of strength that helps their beloved get through difficult times. And if someone even looks at an Eight's partner funny, watch out!

> Eights can be risk takers in general, but they often look for a sure thing in love.
> –Stephanie Barron Hall[1]

Though Eights are risk-takers by nature, committing to love is not always easy for an Eight. Fearing they may be rejected, harmed, or betrayed, it may feel challenging to give another human being that much power over

---

1 Stephanie Barron Hall, *The Enneagram in Love: A Roadmap for Building and Strengthening Romantic Relationships* (Emeryville, CA: Rockridge Press, 2020), 76-78.

them. But love is a high-risk, high-reward decision and Eights never back down from going big.

Today, I want to look at some of the blind spots Eights may have in relationships. Though it won't be easy, this quick flyover will help improve your relationships and prevent future surprises. For guidance, let's turn to 1 Corinthians 13:4-7 and read the apostle Paul's classic chapter on love in his first letter to the Corinthian church.

Love is not arrogant. It is not stubborn and overbearing but flexible and accommodating. Type Eight Meredith Boggs says one time she insisted that her husband clean out the gutters, pressure-wash the deck, and haul the trash to the dump—all within two hours before sunset! Eights can place unreasonable demands on their loved ones.[2] Suzanne Stabile adds that some of the biggest misunderstandings these types have in the home are centered around expectations that haven't been clearly articulated.[3] It may feel burdensome at times to slow down and explain duties that seem obvious, but sometimes the rest of us just need a little help to see all of the things in this world (and our homes) that are out of place.

> **Deep satisfaction in relationships will only come when you show up unguarded.**

Because love is a two-way street, you must humbly drop the self-sufficient persona and make your needs known. Intimacy, after all, is formed through mutual exchanges of care, and it's neither foolish nor weak to ask for help. Humility also means pulling up the shades and allowing others to see your tender heart. Deep satisfaction in relationships will only come when you show up unguarded. While you naturally bring intensity and excitement, you also need to remember that adventures with your partner are not the same thing as building intimacy, which requires you to be daring enough to expose those softer emotions.

Love is not rude. It is being more open-minded and agreeable rather than being blunt, defensive, or bossy. It is resisting the urge to pick a fight about trivial issues to keep things "fun" and intense. Though it may feel natural for you to *test* in

---

2 Boggs, *The Journey Home*, 40-41.
3 Stabile, *The Path Between Us*, 20.

order to *trust*, remember that your confrontational intimacy is foreign to others and may come off as rude or even a strategy for separation.

Love does not insist on its own way. When Eights are unhealthy, they may become controlling, possessive, or badger others to do what they want. When they think they are right, they may brush off their partner's feelings or ideas. Also, their lust for big things and dreams can exhaust their partner or lead to neglect, as they are more prone to overworking than other types.

These blind spots are general for Eights and may not apply to you, but either way, they aren't fun to hear, so let me remind you how much we appreciate you. Defenders motivate their partners to reach their full potential every day. They are exceedingly attentive, generous, romantic, and even secretly sentimental, especially when they use their penchant for deep attentiveness in areas such as gift giving or planning dates and excursions. You come to mind when we hear Paul say that "love rejoices with the truth" and "bears all things, believes all things, hopes all things, endures all things."

The Good News for Defenders is that in the light of Jesus' life of sacrificial love, we can see our blind spots clearly. Through Jesus, the multi-faceted, unfailing love of the triune Godhead described in 1 Corinthians 13 has been made visible to us. Just as a diverse spectrum of bright colors shine through a crystal prism, so too does the patience, kindness, truth, and enduring love of the Father shine through the Son with magnificent glory—and now it shines through you as well.

→ Pray

Father, You have loved me so well. When it comes to loving others with vulnerability, my love sometimes falls short. Help me not to insist on having my way all the time and show my loved ones they are my number one priority. Enable me by Your Holy Spirit to offer others mercy and patience from the well of Your steadfast love, which endures forever.

Day 22 Reflections:

How have you demonstrated God's love through your generosity, protection, and unrelenting devotion?

What do you think would be the worst and the best possible outcomes if you were to openly share all of your feelings and insecurities with a loved one?

Among the blind spots mentioned today, which one do you struggle with the most, and what steps can you take to pay more attention to it?

→ Respond

Read or listen to one of Brené Brown's books, such as Daring Greatly or The Power of Vulnerability. She has made exceptional contributions to the area of vulnerability, which is one of the Eight's significant areas of growth. A vulnerable Eight is a powerful thing!

Day 23:
My Way Or the Highway

And there came a voice to him: "Rise, Peter; kill and eat." But Peter said, "By no means, Lord; for I have never eaten anything that is common or unclean." And the voice came to him again a second time, "What God has made clean, do not call common."

—Acts 10:13-15

FOR CENTURIES, GOD'S CHOSEN PEOPLE HAD ONE identity, set apart as holy among the nations, and their distinctive practices included a strict dietary code. *Clean* foods were allowed, *unclean* ones were not. But as the early church expanded beyond its Jewish roots, the issue of food became a recurring challenge.

> **There's more than one way to skin a cat.**
> –English Proverb

In a famous episode from the book of Acts, the apostle Peter had a transformative experience. During a prayerful trance, a sheet from heaven descended, carrying both clean and unclean animals, and God said, "Rise, Peter; kill and eat."[1] This moment marked a shift in God's plan, embracing a more inclusive diet to welcome Gentiles into the faith. Peter, rooted

---

1 Acts 10:9-15

in the traditional *Hebrew* way, found it challenging to accept this new approach, especially after considering it the "right way" for so long.

Like Peter, who went so far as to *challenge God* on the dietary issue, unhealthy Eights see their truth as *the* truth, and it's not hard to see why. Eights are usually the "top dog" wherever they go. Being the loudest and often holding positions of authority gives you more power to define what's "right" in a given situation. Also, Eights live in the real, concrete world, think pragmatically, and perceive things more directly with their senses, which leaves them believing they have *objective facts* while others only have *subjective opinions*.

It's advantageous to have a black-and-white worldview because nuancing takes precious time and slows things down. Also, you look stronger when you can state something with absolute certainty as opposed to communicating in more gray tones, which may make you look uncertain and weak.[2] Here's the thing: overconfidence is not a strength but a chink in the Eight's armor.

Eights need to shift their paradigm from "my way or the highway" to "my way *or* your way." Before you say something loud enough to convince others of your truth (or even try and convince yourself), say these words: *I could be wrong*. Remind yourself that not everything can be categorized neatly as good

> God still sees you as strong even when you're dead wrong.

or evil. In fact, much of life is deciding between two competing *good* values. As an Eight, it will be immensely helpful in the future to realize that others with opposing views might actually be defending another *good* value, and that it may be you who is trying to fit your square peg of a value into the round hole of someone else's context. Slow down, take a breath, stay curious, and seek to learn more about where others are coming from.

Another bit of advice is not to reframe every "conviction" as a serious justice issue. Pastor Andrew Wilson categorizes truth into three categories: blood (core convictions worth fighting for), ink (important beliefs but subject to change),

---

2 Cron and Stabile, *The Road Back to You*, 47.

and pencil (opinions that are easily erasable).³ The path of growth for you will include doing the hard work of distinguishing between blood, ink, and pencil issues (theological and otherwise), and then choosing not to hold them all with equal weight, which can lead to a reputation for fighting the wrong battles and creating mountains out of molehills. Stand up for the things that actually matter but seek to live graciously open-handed with as much as possible, allowing others to have their way.

The Good News for Defenders is you don't have to fight for your truth because "the truth will set you free."⁴ Like Peter, you can relax your defenses and allow God to show you a vision of a more colorful, delicious world. In the end, compromising actually speeds things up rather than slowing them down. When Peter finally let go of his black-and-white thinking, his judgment toward the Gentiles subsided, his gospel witness accelerated, and he enjoyed a new and exciting fellowship with these brothers and sisters in Christ. Therefore, for your sake and the health of your relationships, allow doubt to creep into your certainty and acknowledge that you don't have to be right all the time. God still sees you as strong even when you're dead wrong. So, the next time you want to get on that soapbox, look at the person in front of you and ask yourself, "Would I rather be right or be effective?"

→ Pray

Father, I want Your way and not my way. Help me live out my convictions with boldness and my opinions with gentleness. This is extremely difficult, but I know Your Holy Spirit will guide me with truth and grace. Free me from my narrow way of seeing the world by giving me an open-hearted curiosity to eagerly explore new perspectives.

---

3   Andrew Wilson, "Pencil, Ink and Blood," Think Theology, September 10, 2012, https://thinktheology.co.uk/blog/article/pencil-ink-and-blood.

4   John 8:32

Day 23 Reflections:

What don't you like about living in the gray? What do you fear will happen?

How has "my way or the highway" behavior led to unnecessary stress, strained relationships, or missed opportunities?

Where in your life (or theology) do you need to learn to be more open-handed, flexible, nuanced, or compromising?

→ Respond

Question your assumptions. When you encounter something new or unfamiliar, resist the urge to immediately judge it as good or bad. Instead, gather more information, analyze the context, avoid extremes, and look for any middle ground.

Day 24:
Navigating Denial

Trust in the LORD with all your heart, and do not lean on your own understanding. In all your ways acknowledge him, and he will make straight your paths.

—Proverbs 3:5-6

IN THE EARLY TWENTIETH CENTURY, WHEN THE only method of transatlantic travel was still by ship, the *Titanic* stood out as a marvel of engineering. Hailed as unsinkable, this massive pleasure-cruiser-people-mover was the paragon of both class and safety. However, despite the owners' and crew's confidence, its maiden voyage ended in tragedy. Like the *Titanic*, Defenders are truly marvelous to behold and appear to have an unsinkable reputation. But their overconfidence can sometimes blind them to the hidden dangers lurking beneath the surface.

> He who can no longer listen to his brother will soon be no longer listening to God either.
>
> –Dietrich Bonhoeffer[1]

In life, we often encounter "icebergs"— hidden challenges and vulnerabilities that, if left unacknowledged, can lead

---

1 Dietrich Bonhoeffer, *Life Together*, tr. John W. Doberstein (New York: Harper & Brothers Publishers, 1954), 97-98.

to shipwrecks. The story of the *Titanic* is a warning that denial can lead to disaster—an important lesson considering *denial* is the Eight's primary defense mechanism. We define denial as the dismissal of inconvenient or painful truths that don't fit into the Eight's way of seeing things. Unlike Type Fours—who may sometimes dwell too long on their emotional "icebergs," plumbing the depths of each feeling, and inspecting each personal vulnerability (real or perceived) under a microscope—Eights tend to take the opposite approach, pushing unwanted realities out of sight and out of mind.

Denial can take the form of pretending you aren't physically sick, even though you may have a high fever telling you otherwise. While most kids say, "Ouch," after a fall or complain to an adult when getting picked on by older siblings, you'll hear my Eight son saying, "That didn't hurt." One time, he crashed his bike, and (an X-ray later revealed) punctured a small hole in his intestine. Because he didn't complain or shed tears, the only cue we had to take him to the emergency room was that he started to turn completely white.

Denial can also take the form of ignoring emotional needs by masking feelings of sadness or fear with anger or aggression. In the workplace, Eights may face criticism or setbacks but deny the impact on them by responding with statements such as "Their opinion doesn't matter," or "I don't care what they think." Eights may downplay the emotional toll that conflict has had on them saying, "It didn't affect me that much," or by dismissing the impact of past traumatic experiences and the need for therapy saying, "I've dealt with it already." ("Dealt with it" often means: *pushed it down and forgotten about it.*)

> **Denial can lead to disaster.**

The Eight trap, according to Beatrice Chestnut, is that "avoiding vulnerability leaves you vulnerable."[2] Motivated to feel strong and in control, they may not take threats seriously or consider their natural human limitations, creating situations that leave them even more prone to danger. When unhealthy Eights keep moving on the path of denial, they may become insensitive to the discomfort of shame and guilt, leading them to become more calloused toward others.[3]

---

[2] Chestnut, *The Complete Enneagram*.

[3] Claudio Naranjo, *Character and Neurosis: An Integrative View* (Nevada City, CA: Gateways/IDHHB, 1994), 146-147.

Remember, reality is your friend, not a foe. You are wonderful at facing reality and conquering it when it shows up in the world outside, so learning to identify and face it head-on in your internal world will keep you from sinking. Like the *Titanic* captain, the next time you receive a warning call from someone else, take it more seriously—especially considering the fact that you probably *are* someone's captain right now and have decision-making power. The whole crew and ship are relying on you. Be patient enough to listen to your trusted advisors and humble enough to listen to those who disagree with you, knowing there's a grain of truth in every criticism.

The Good News for Defenders is that if you listen to the Lord and don't lean on your own understanding of how things are, He will protect you from "icebergs" and keep you going full steam ahead. He wants to keep you from deception, both from the world *and* from your internal voice. The apostle Paul exhorted the Corinthian church to avoid self-deception by considering yourself a "fool" instead of "wise" in your own eyes.[4] Adopt the wisdom of Socrates who said, "I know that I am intelligent, because I know that I know nothing"[5] and seek to find opportunities to be vulnerable, sharing your areas of unknowing and even fear with those you love and trust.

→ Pray

Father, teach me to balance my strength with vulnerability and to listen to wise counsel. Thank You for Your promise of protection and guidance. Grant me the discernment to distinguish between confidence and overconfidence and the strength to face uncomfortable truths. Keep me on the path of wisdom and away from the dangers of denial.

---

4 1 Corinthians 3:18
5 Arun Tiwari, *Socrates: A Complete Biography* (New Delhi, India: Prabhat Prakashan, 2023).

Day 24 Reflections:

How do you relate to denial as a defense mechanism? When have you noticed yourself putting inconvenient or painful truths out of sight or out of mind?

What are the "icebergs" in your life that you've been avoiding or denying? Take time to pray and ask God to reveal these hidden vulnerabilities.

To avoid the disasters of denial, what can you do to become more of a receptive person?

→ Respond

Embrace active listening. Create a safe space for others to speak without interruption. This encourages them to form their own opinions and speak up confidently, especially when they feel they can't match your intensity.

Day 25:

The Strong Shepherd

Even though I walk through the valley of the shadow of death, I will fear no evil, for you are with me; your rod and your staff, they comfort me.

—Psalm 23:4

THE BIBLE CAN BE OFFENSIVE AT TIMES. For instance, instead of using mighty creatures like lions, tigers, or bears, God chose the metaphor of *sheep* to describe His people. These fluffy creatures are vulnerable, not overly intelligent, hard to manage, prone to wander, and easily frightened. They depend entirely on a shepherd to keep them safe from predators and just pure dumb mistakes. Does this strike a chord?

The good news, as we see in Psalm 23, is that we have a powerful Shepherd—not the soft, "sweater-robe" type depicted in some religious art, but the kind who wields an iron rod to defend us against predators. Ancient shepherds, like young King David, were like the cowboys of their time. They wandered into the wilderness, wielding those rods and slings with

> Speak softly and carry a big stick.
>
> –Theodore Roosevelt[1]

---

1 National Geographic Society. "Big Stick Diplomacy." Big Stick Diplomacy, October 19, 2023. https://education.nationalgeographic.org/resource/big-stick-diplomacy/.

deadly force, fiercely protecting their flocks against the dangers of lions, bears, and thieves.[2] That's my shepherd!

Yet, despite being a strong protector, David chose to portray himself as a sheep beginning with, "The Lord is my shepherd; I shall not want."[3] The next line is equally important: "He makes me lie down in green pastures."[4] Notice that the Lord didn't ask; He *made* David lie down. Getting someone like an Eight to relax can be quite a feat, as they are constantly pursuing action, excitement, and confrontation. But that's not what our Shepherd is after: He wants to restore your soul.

Eventually, God invites mature sheep to become shepherds themselves, entrusted with the care of others. This is where healthy Eights shine. They become heroes like David, stepping up in times of need, shouldering responsibility for their people. What's even more remarkable is that Eights not only lead their tribes but also accept the consequences of their collective mistakes. This quality in Eights points us to Jesus, who willingly sacrificed Himself, not for His own errors, but for ours. The Good Shepherd lays down His life for His sheep.

> The Good Shepherd stays awake, watching over you until the dawn breaks.

Similarly, Eights will step in front of a train, catch a grenade, or do anything for the people in their inner-circle. When he was three years old, my son Zeke literally climbed up a tall eight-year-old like a tree and ripped the glasses off his head after he made fun of our five year old son, Zane. Nothing upsets Zeke more than when *his* people are insulted or attacked. Yet, this tough-as-nails child doesn't just defend others; he shares snacks and popsicles from our pantry and freezer with the younger children at the playground, whom he considers his responsibility to care for and shield.

Eights often assume the role of a protective parent, becoming more tender and open when interacting with children, grandchildren, or animals. It is truly

---

2   1 Samuel 17:34-36

3   Psalm 23:1

4   Psalm 23:2

admirable seeing Eights in this role when they are like "a mother tiger gingerly carrying her cubs in her powerful jaws."[5] They'll go to great lengths to ensure the safety and happiness of their innocent ones. When healthy Eights bring this same level of sacrificial care to their spouses, workplaces, or churches, their leadership becomes exponentially impactful. Our world doesn't need more distant leaders who crave the spotlight but more compassionate shepherds who are so close to their flock that they smell like sheep.

The Good News for Defenders is you can say, "Even though I walk through the valley of the shadow of death, I will fear no evil, for you are with me; your rod and your staff, they comfort me."[6] You don't have to stay awake all night, being alert for predators. The Good Shepherd stays awake, watching over you until the dawn breaks. As David sings in the fourth Psalm, "In peace I will both lie down and sleep; for you alone, O Lord, make me dwell in safety."[7]

As a shepherd-leader after the model of our Messiah, Jesus has given you all authority on heaven and earth to pick up your staff today and call out sin, confront false religion, protest injustice, and tell the wolves in sheep's clothing where to go. Because God did not give you a Spirit of fear, but of power,[8] it is up to you to step into your authority, loving others with your protective presence and sacrificial love.

→ Pray

Father, show me just how dependent I am as one of Your sheep. Even as I learn to be vulnerable with others, I know I can always lie down in your peaceful pastures. Thank You for being my powerful Shepherd, always ready to defend and protect, even in the watches of the night. I'm grateful for the opportunity to be a shepherd to others. May my leadership be characterized by sacrificial care, bringing safety and joy to those I serve.

---

5   Wagner, *Nine Lenses on the World*, 432-433.
6   Psalm 23:4
7   Psalm 4:8
8   2 Timothy 1:7

Day 25 Reflections:

How do you feel about being called a sheep? What insights do you learn about yourself from this metaphor?

When has God made you lie down in green pastures against your will? What can you do to incorporate moments of stillness into your daily routine?

How does the imagery of a rod help you discern your responsibilities as a spiritual shepherd? When have you had to protect your sheep from "wolves in sheep's clothing"?

→ Respond

Dedicate a specific time each day for a few minutes of quiet reflection in a peaceful spot. It could be in the morning, during a lunch break, or before bed. Let go of control, reflect on your vulnerability, pray for discernment, and practice gratitude.

Day 26:

Lion and the Lamb

And one of the elders said to me, "Weep no more; behold, the Lion of the tribe of Judah, the Root of David, has conquered, so that he can open the scroll and its seven seals." And between the throne and the four living creatures and among the elders I saw a Lamb standing, as though it had been slain.

—Revelation 5:5-6a

AT EIGHTEEN, AGNES JOINED THE ENGLISH LADIES, a teaching order of nuns. She later taught geography in Calcutta, India, but was drawn to a slum behind the school. As the school's director, she began caring for the sick in the slum, and she left the convent in 1946 to live among the poor. Today, thousands follow her example, taking vows of chastity, poverty, and obedience to serve the poorest of the poor.[2]

> **The best ministry you might do today is to listen to someone's pain all the way to the bottom.**
>
> –David Matthis[1]

---

1 David Matthis, "Six Lessons in Good Listening," Desiring God, April 3, 2014, https://www.desiringgod.org/articles/six-lessons-in-good-listening.
2 Rohr and Ebert, *The Enneagram*, 131.

Agnes, who we now know as Mother Teresa, presented all of the mature qualities of a Two; however, due largely to her strength and dogged pursuit of justice, many are convinced she was an Eight. She fought for the "widows and orphans" of our day—the most unsupported, neglected group of people on the planet—setting up hospices on the street saying, "They have lived like animals. They should at least die like human beings."[3] She advocated for the neglected and the outcasts, serving those named by their home culture as literally "untouchable"; she challenged leaders around the world to stop talking about helping their poor and downtrodden and actually do something about it—even challenging the German prime minister in 1982 to accept refugees into the country.

Mother Teresa was both tough *and* tender, the kind of leader all Defenders should aspire to be. Eights can be perceived by others as lacking sensitivity because of their default stance, which accentuates their stronger attributes and masks their more vulnerable emotions. They are like eggs—hard on the outside but soft and yielding on the inside.[4] Showing your soft side to others may sound unappetizing, I know, but it's absolutely required to find success in relationships and at work. It is *the* thing that Eights need to work on the most to make people feel more connected to and want to follow you.[5]

> Becoming more tender doesn't make you less tough.

When Eights travel on the growth path line to Type Two, they *build* bridges rather than burn them, temper their justice with mercy, become givers not takers, move toward others rather than against them, and "learn the power of love rather than being obsessed with the love of power."[6] The healthiest of Eights quite simply think of themselves less and observe the needs of others more, shouldering them on their backs as if they were their own. They acquire a softer, kinder, and more approachable demeanor, and their trademark truthfulness is seasoned with a lot of grace (even if it tastes underwhelming at first).

---

3 Feldmann, *Träume beginnen zu leben*, 86.

4 Matthew Stephen Brown, *A Book Called YOU: Understanding the Enneagram from a Grace-Filled, Biblical Perspective* (Nashville, TN: W Publishing, 2021), 155.

5 Stabile, *The Path Between Us*, 37-38.

6 Riso and Hudson, *Personality Types*, 331-332.

Don't stop your "love through doing" approach, which is actually solving the world's greatest problems right now—but don't forget to also develop the art of "love through listening," which will make you even more effective. As God's image-bearers, we are called to not only represent His hands and feet but His ears and heart also, meaning you should be "quick to hear, slow to speak, slow to anger"[7] as the apostle James commands. Unhealthy Eights can be a bit tone deaf to others' feelings, but healthy Eights listen very closely to try to pick up the frequencies of others' subtle fears and emotions. Through listening and empathy, we invite others to understand just how much they matter to us.

The Good News for Defenders is becoming more tender doesn't make you less tough. One of the great paradoxes of John's vision recorded in Revelation is that Jesus is both a Lion and a Lamb. How is it that the mighty and powerful One who lays waste to His enemies is also gentle and lowly? How is it that the meek Lamb, not a strong military victor, is the One who conquers and overcomes? Because the victory of the cross is one of sacrificial love.

And yet, it's also true that Jesus being a Lamb doesn't make Him any less of a Lion. As C. S. Lewis writes in the *The Lion, The Witch, and The Wardrobe*, Aslan, the ruler of Narnia, is a great lion. Susan, after hearing the shocking news that he is not a man, tells Mr. Beaver, "I shall feel rather nervous about meeting a lion." She then asks Mr. Beaver if Aslan is safe. Mr. Beaver replies, "Safe? Who said anything about safe? 'Course he isn't safe. But he's good. He's the King."[8]

→ Pray

Father, give me the strength to be both tough and tender. Thank You for examples like Mother Teresa, who became an unforgettable heroine, not by exalting herself, but by becoming a humble servant like Your Son, Jesus. Help me to be filled with that kind of selfless compassion and understand that my true strength as a leader lies in empathy.

---

7 James 1:19

8 Liz Wann. "Always Good, Never Safe." Desiring God, March 30, 2017. http://www.desiringgod.org/articles/always-good-never-safe.

Day 26 Reflections:

What qualities in Mother Teresa's life and work do you see in yourself?

How does the paradox of Jesus being a Lion and a Lamb challenge you today? How can you embody both qualities in your leadership style?

When you have caught yourself being "tone-deaf" to others' emotions? What can you do to put yourself in someone else's shoes and feel what they are feeling?

> ### → Respond
>
> Cultivate tenderness by spending time with the most vulnerable, like a child or beloved pet. Embrace them in your arms, allowing the physical closeness to evoke tenderness within your heart as you let your guard down.[9]

---

9 Moser, *The Enneagram of Discernment*, 184.

Day 27:

Knockout Punch

So I do not run aimlessly; I do not box as one beating the air. But I discipline my body and keep it under control, lest after preaching to others I myself should be disqualified.

—1 Corinthians 9:26-27

IN A SMALL, GRITTY BOXING GYM, THERE once was a young fighter named Jake. He was known for being methodical and disciplined. He looked different from his peers who were much bigger and stronger. One day, while sparring against the best boxer in the gym, Jake's disciplined approach paid off. While his impressive opponent aimed for a quick win by delivering countless jabs, Jake remained calm and self-controlled, focusing on precision and technique. In the final round, Jake seized the perfect moment to deliver a knockout punch, winning the fight and demonstrating that true strength comes from patient discipline, not brute force.

> Go ahead. Make my day.
>
> –Harry Callahan (Clint Eastwood)[1]

The apostle Paul imparted a comparable spiritual lesson to the Corinthian church, emphasizing that

---

1   David Sterritt, *The Cinema of Clint Eastwood: Chronicles of America* (New York, NY: Columbia University Press, 2014), 127.

rather than aimlessly shadowboxing, he kept his body under control to ensure he wouldn't miss out on the prize.

Defenders often have a "ready, fire, aim" approach to life. As Ian Cron explains, "Because anger is so easy for them to access, an average Eight can be a little too quick to the draw, firing off a few rounds at people without thinking beforehand about the consequences."[2] Additionally, Eights often ask what they need to *do* before they ask themselves how they should *feel*. This is because momentum is everything to an Eight—but feelings are not aerodynamic. Yes, sometimes anger or frustration may spur you to action, but emotions like fear and pain or joy or sorrow need space to breathe to fully wash over you.

Your energy is motivating for those of us who need to get off our rear and "just do it." As Paul told the Roman church, "Do not be slothful in zeal, be fervent in spirit, serve the Lord."[3] Defenders are more zealous than anyone I know, but the caveat is that an "act now, think later" mentality will not always serve you in life. That's why Type Eight Meredith Boggs tries to slow down the speed at which she does everything: "In slowing down, I am able to listen, learn, and respond instead of react. Slowing down with the simple things—how fast I talk, how quickly I eat, and yes, even how fast I drive—creates a physical margin for stillness to enter."[4]

> **Defenders often have a "ready, fire, aim" approach to life.**

Unhealthy Eights can't help but react when they encounter incompetence or unfairness, and they don't always respond with the best words. Confrontation provides a quick tension release, making discomfort dissipate and giving them peace of mind. However, the aftermath after this cathartic release can be surprising, with Eights believing they've resolved the tension, only to face unexpected relational consequences—all because they didn't pause and think, "Why am I angry? Who's actually to blame for this?"[5]

---

2 Cron and Stabile, *The Road Back to You*, 45.

3 Romans 12:11

4 Boggs, *The Journey Home*, 46-47.

5 Helen Palmer, The Enneagram in Love and Work: Understanding Your Intimate and Business Relationships (New York, NY: HarperOne, 2010), 215.

Healthy Eights must learn to become *witnesses* and *advocates,* not judges. Judgment is all too often an emotional reaction, whereas patient observation takes discipline. Witnesses observe the differences between two parties and the contexts in which they are shaped before responding. Advocates, like the Holy Spirit, listen to the feelings beneath the surface that show up in a person's words or actions. Then they speak up or act to bring the best possible outcome for all involved.

To access Christ's spirit of self-control, you can begin thinking like a healthy Type Five, which will help you live "mindfully instead of mindlessly."[6] A Five's strategy includes *thinking* before doing, *analysis* before action, and being *proactive* over reactive. Like a Five, create a "thinking gap" to engage in more mental activity, observation, research, and planning before reacting, along with making a special effort to forecast how every response will impact your relationships.

The Good News for Defenders is that Jesus delivered a knockout punch to Satan not by charging hell with a squirt gun but through the discipline of a focused athlete, keeping His body under control through His sufferings, so as to win the prize of redemption for all of mankind. And we have that same spirit: "for God gave us a spirit not of fear but of power and love and self-control."[7] The addition of self-control to that list makes all the difference!

→ Pray

Father, I need Your strength and self-control. Help me pause before reacting, respond wisely, be a witness, and then be an advocate instead of a judge. Give me the discipline to wield my power for good, just as Jesus did. Today, I will embrace the wisdom of thinking before acting and proactively consider the impact of my actions on others.

---

6 Ian Morgan Cron, *The Story of You: An Enneagram Journey to Becoming Your True Self* (New York, NY: HarperCollins, 2021), 45.

7 2 Timothy 1:7

Day 27 Reflections:

How has your experience been when you've channeled your inner "Jake," practicing discipline and focus instead of engaging in "shadowboxing" in your life?

Think about a recent situation where you reacted impulsively instead of responding thoughtfully. What consequences might have come from taking a more patient and observant approach?

How can you apply the principles of becoming a witness and advocate, as opposed to a judge, in your interactions with others?

> ### → Respond
>
> It can be valuable to pause briefly before engaging in conversation or making important choices. Going for a relaxing walk can be especially beneficial, particularly during times of heightened anger or intense emotions.[8]

---

8 Chestnut and Paes, *The Enneagram Guide to Waking Up*, 216.

Day 28:
The Loneliness of Leadership

And I will come down and talk with you there. And I will take some of the

Spirit that is on you and put it on them, and they shall bear the burden

of the people with you, so that you may not bear it yourself alone.

—Numbers 11:17

LEGENDARY BOXER MUHAMMAD ALI—KNOWN AS MUCH FOR his larger-than-life personality as for his extraordinary skills in the ring—reiterated a profound perspective on leadership from his own experience that likely resonates with fellow Defenders: "The strongest person in the world is also the loneliest."[2]

As an Eight, you know the solitary path often associated with leadership: you don't necessarily seek these positions in everything, but it comes naturally due to your confidence and ability to take charge. People constantly looking to you for direction can be isolating, leaving you to bear the weight of leadership without feeling permission to express your challenges and fears. Constantly

> The strongest man in the world is he who stands most alone.
>
> –Henrik Ibsen[1]

---

1   Henrik Ibsen, *An Enemy Of The People* (New York, NY: G&D Media, 2022), 188.
2   Wagner, *Nine Lenses on the World*, 422.

having leadership thrust on you like this can ultimately insulate you from deep connection, love, and feeling truly understood.[3]

On Day 16, we discussed how Moses' stress led to a major meltdown before the entire nation. What we didn't address was the lonely journey of leadership that led to that point. The book of Numbers in the Old Testament could be retitled as *In the Shadow of Leadership: Moses' Dark Night of the Soul*.

The shadow over Moses' leadership grew darker when even his own family members, Aaron and Miriam, doubted and turned against him.[4] It's incredibly lonely when division arises within your family or team due to your calling. Have you experienced people close to you doubting or criticizing you without understanding the weight of leadership or seeing the big picture? Despite this, when Moses' sister was afflicted with leprosy for disrespecting the Lord's anointed, Moses chose mercy over revenge—a lesson all Eights can learn from.

> You're not the only one who feels like no one else cares.

However, even private family squabbles turning public wasn't the most difficult part. Moses' true breaking point came when the Israelites rejected him, weeping and begging to return to Egypt. At least you have never had such a crisis of confidence that your team wanted to return to literal slavery! Imagine Moses' feelings of betrayal at that moment. Yet he didn't seek vengeance, but instead prayed for the people's forgiveness, displaying why he was called the most humble man on the face of the planet.

Every hero in the Bible experienced the loneliness of leadership. You're not the only one who feels like no one else cares. When Elijah fled into the wilderness, he was flooded with grief that he was the only follower of Yahweh left. But in a gentle whisper, God revealed that there were still seven thousand in Israel who had not bowed their knees to Baal.[5] David had many lonely years and recorded these experiences in his Psalms while living behind enemy lines on the run from King Saul. The Son of God Himself was misunderstood by His own people, and

---

3   Case, *The Honest Enneagram*, 196.
4   Numbers 12:1-2
5   1 Kings 19:18

His disciples left Him alone as He prayed on the night He was betrayed. Talk about a dark night of the soul!

The Good News for Defenders is that you are never truly alone. When promising to provide co-leaders who would come alongside him, God told Moses, "And I will come down and talk with you there. And I will take some of the Spirit that is on you and put it on them, and they shall bear the burden of the people with you, so that you may not bear it yourself alone."[6] The next time you feel lonely; even when you can't see it or feel it, take comfort in the knowledge that God is with you, guiding you through the desert like Moses and equipping you to face the challenges of leadership with faith and courage—even when you're surrounded by a bunch of complainers. He's got your back!

Seasons of loneliness and depression will come like waves, rising, washing over you, and then returning to the sea. But the sun will always break through eventually, and when it does, you will emerge from your dark night of the soul like a phoenix rising from the ashes. As Dr. Elisabeth Kubler-Ross says, "The most beautiful people we have known are those who have known defeat, known suffering, known struggle, known loss, and have found their way out of the depths. ... Beautiful people do not just happen."[7]

→ Pray

Father, help me respond with mercy and humility in the face of challenges like Moses did. I find comfort in knowing other heroes like Elijah, David, and Your Son, Jesus, knew the loneliness of leadership. In times of loneliness and despair, remind me that the sun will eventually break through as I hold onto the promise of Your constant presence.

---

6   Numbers 11:17
7   Calhoun and Loughrige, *Spiritual Rhythms*, 109.

Day 28 Reflections:

How do Muhammad Ali's words from the beginning of today's devotion resonate with your leadership journey?

_____
_____
_____
_____

When have you faced a situation where those close to you doubted or criticized your leadership? How did you respond? How does Moses' responses to betrayal challenge you?

_____
_____
_____
_____

Reflect on the idea that beautiful people emerge from struggles and adversity. How have your challenges and experiences shaped you as a leader and as a person?

_____
_____
_____
_____

> ### → Respond
>
> Consider joining or forming a leadership peer group or mastermind with other leaders in your industry or community. This group can serve as a safe space for sharing experiences, challenges, and advice.

Day 29:
Betrayed with a Kiss

While he was still speaking, there came a crowd, and the man called Judas, one of the twelve, was leading them. He drew near to Jesus to kiss him, but Jesus said to him, "Judas, would you betray the Son of Man with a kiss?"

—Luke 22:47-48

IN THE SHADOWY DEPTHS OF GETHSEMANE'S GARDEN, an electrifying act of betrayal transpired. As Jesus knelt in fervent prayer, grappling with the conflict between His very human will and His heavenly Father's, His closest disciples lay on the ground, slumbering in ignorance. Meanwhile Judas, who had been granted the privilege of being by Jesus' side, had slipped away and brought the authorities to arrest his Master, betraying his intimate Companion with that sign of intimate love—a kiss. In that infamous, pivotal moment, we get a glimpse of the depths to which trust can be exploited.

> True friends stab you in the front.
>
> —Oscar Wilde[1]

You can begin to see why Eights are tempted to believe the lie: *It's not okay to trust anyone.* As therapist and author Dan Allender admits, "If you lead, you will eventually serve with Judas or

---

1 Chestnut, *The Complete Enneagram.*

Peter."[2] This hard-hitting reality is why I think many Eights live with a low-grade, often unconscious, paranoia about being betrayed. If you ask an Eight to tell you what their fears are, you'll often get a blank stare; however, the fear of betrayal frequently simmers just beneath the surface.

An unidentified or denied fear can leave room for unhealthy coping mechanisms. For example, in the Self-Preservation Eights, this fear may manifest as an overdependence on money, looking at it as "one of the few things they can depend on to feel self-sufficient. It is the source of their security and independence."[3] For Social Eights, however, as my friend Catherine Bell explains, this may manifest less as physical acquisition and more as collecting friends in high places who can serve as "off-ramps" in case they are betrayed.

While there are plenty of stories in the Bible (and possibly from your own lived experience) to validate this fear of betrayal, it's equally true that there might *not* be a Judas in your home or in the workplace right now. As Suzanne Stabile explains,

> Many Eights live with low-grade, often unconscious, paranoia about being betrayed.

"When [Eights are] in stress, they make up scenarios where those around them are being disloyal or dishonest, which is usually not the case. An example would be an Eight deciding that someone or a group is an enemy and attacking them before they are attacked or betrayed."[4]

This is why in her workshops, Stabile attempts to help Eights heal by discerning if they have actually been betrayed in a given situation. As she listens patiently to examples of how others have been underhanded or disloyal, she often replies, "I wouldn't call that betrayal—don't you think it could have been a mistake?"[5] This helpful reframing of the situation can help Eights release their suspicions and gain back some of their peaceful sanity.

---

2   Dan B. Allender, *Leading With a Limp: Turning Your Struggles Into Strengths* (Colorado Springs, CO: Waterbrook Press, 2006), 31.

3   Riso and Hudson, *Personality Types*, 320-321.

4   Suzanne Stabile, *The Journey Toward Wholeness: Enneagram Wisdom for Stress, Balance, and Transformation* (Downers Grove, IL: InterVarsity Press, 2021), 105-106.

5   Stabile, *The Path Between Us*, 27.

The Good News for Defenders is that you will never be betrayed by God.[6] As you learn to replace the uncertainty of others' past or potential betrayals with the surety of Christ's protection, you will experience improved relationships and reduced stress, allowing you to open your heart and take more risks in connecting and collaborating with others. And in those moments (which will likely happen in truth at some point) when you are truly betrayed, don't respond in anger, as Peter did, going so far as to arm himself and attempt to kill one of his Messiah's captors. In that moment of fear, anger, and confusion, Jesus disarmed Peter, reminding him that, while the Son of God could call on an army of angels, his actions would only put a stop to the plan of redemption that was unfolding.[7]

The lesson for Peter (and all Eights) is to recognize that seeking revenge or reacting in anger or fear can obstruct the path to healing and new life. God is fulfilling His plan in your life, and you mustn't allow acts of betrayal to divert you onto an ineffective detour. Just as Jesus did not make a mistake in choosing Judas as a disciple and was not surprised by his betrayal, you too can endure the most severe betrayals, knowing God is in control and His plan will prevail.

→ Pray

Father, thank You for Your unwavering faithfulness and the assurance of Your protection. Teach me to trust again, discerning between loyalty and honest mistakes. In moments of betrayal, help me resist revenge and choose to continue on the path of redemption. I trust in Your sovereignty, knowing Your plan will prevail.

---

[6] Deuteronomy 31:8
[7] Matthew 26:52-54

Day 29 Reflections:

When did you start to believe the lie "It's not okay to trust anyone?" What people or life experiences have reinforced that belief?

Take a moment to reflect on your anticipation of being rejected. Do you find yourself frequently feeling the need to act in certain ways just to prevent potential rejection?

Are there instances in your life where you may have misjudged an action as betrayal when it could have been a mistake or miscommunication? How can you take proactive steps to avoid this in the future?

> ### → Respond
>
> Take a moment to reflect on a situation where you've felt betrayed. Consider whether this situation might have been due to a misunderstanding, mistake, or miscommunication rather than a deliberate betrayal.

Day 30:

The Volcano of Emotions

He was despised and rejected by men, a man of sorrows and acquainted with grief; and as one from whom men hide their faces he was despised, and we esteemed him not.

—Isaiah 53:3

IN THE VAST LANDSCAPE OF THE HUMAN heart, there exists a force of nature. Like a volcano, lying quietly until subterranean pressures cause the very earth itself to rupture, this bedrock emotional experience for Defenders can be powerful, fiery, and impossible to ignore. Unfortunately, this foundational aspect of their nature is also one of the most misunderstood—by others and Eights themselves. This visible eruption, full of smoke and ash, that obscures our vision and often masks what lies beneath, is *anger*.

> **Eights aren't afraid to feel—they're afraid their feelings will betray them.**
> –Suzanne Stabile[1]

One of two experiences can be said for Eights: either they categorize *every* emotion as anger—the whole color wheel is stained red—or they almost *never* categorize it as such—red is the one color underlying everything but never

---

1 Stabile, *The Path Between Us*, 27.

allowed to be seen. Some Eights say they quite literally wake up impatient or irritated on a daily basis but don't know why.[2] My friend Kyle, for instance, says that when he is triggered it feels like everything in his field of vision turns red. My son Zeke had a similar experience with grief at the loss of a beloved family pet. While my oldest son cried, Zeke, my little Eight got angry. This "body-based" type experiences emotions intensely, as a rush of energy coursing through their body, but underneath the molten lava that others experience as "anger" is often a deeper layer of emotion such as fear, sadness, vulnerability, insecurity, and disappointment.[3] These emotions, though concealed, buried, or misunderstood, are an essential part of the rich landscape within the tender heart of every Eight.

When Eights are unhealthy, they don't take the time to explore what lies beneath their anger—particularly if its expression causes pain or fear in others. Just as a volcano leaves hidden chambers underground after an eruption, you must venture into these hidden chambers with a lantern, shedding light on the softer, more vulnerable feelings you might have overlooked. As you delve deeper into these recesses, you'll develop a higher emotional intelligence like a Type Four, regularly exploring the causes and aftereffects of their emotions.

> [Eights] categorize every emotion as anger—the whole color wheel is stained red—or they almost never categorize it as such.

Eights have expressed that this basic posture of repressing their feelings leads them to believe their emotions are completely absent—until one day they explode all at once and take them (and anyone in the blast radius) completely by surprise. When this happens, these unexpected emotions may leave you feeling raw and exposed.[4] Overpowering and uncontrollable tears, for example, will confuse you and maybe even lead to a fear that others will attack in your moment of weakness.

According to Suzanne Stabile, Eights sometimes think of themselves as being emotionally expressive because of their natural passion and intensity, but the

---

2   Chestnut, The Complete Enneagram.
3   Chestnut, *The 9 Types of Leadership*, 257-258.
4   Stabile, *The Journey Toward Wholeness*, 192-193.

truth is that often an Eight's passion or expressed anger is just masquerading as deep emotions. Passion is a true gift to us all, but Eights need to make sure it doesn't become a substitute for other feelings that need to be explored and expressed.[5]

Jesus was a kaleidoscope of emotions, able to express (and accurately categorize) the entire spectrum of human warmth and love, anger and frustration, grief and loss. He was not stoic and invincible but fully human, feeling deep compassion toward the sick and infirm, anger toward evil and hypocrisy, grief over death and loneliness, and distress over humanity's waywardness. A "man of sorrows and acquainted with grief,"[6] Jesus was fully in touch with His emotions, making Him relatable, approachable, and someone we could identify with.

The Good News for Defenders is that *all* of our emotions are never far from us, if we will let them in. Remember, embracing your emotions as an Eight is a sign of strength, not weakness. Developing emotional intelligence, the ability to understand and manage your feelings, will amplify your impact as a friend, lover, and leader. Like a skilled painter, your emotions are the vibrant colors that enrich your canvas. Fear, sadness, and hurt, when acknowledged and expressed, add depth to your leadership.

> **→ Pray**
>
> Father, give me wisdom to discern between my passion and genuine emotions, much like how Jesus expressed the entire spectrum of feelings. Guide me in becoming more emotionally multi-dimensional, allowing me to be a more approachable and relatable presence in the lives of those around me.

---

5 Stabile, *The Path Between Us*, 26.
6 Isaiah 53:3

Day 30 Reflections:

Can you recall a specific moment when you, like Zeke, might have initially experienced sadness as anger? How did you navigate that experience?

Which of these emotions do you find challenging to openly experience: sadness, fear, loneliness, insecurity, shame, helplessness, or anxiety? What makes these emotions seem unsettling at first glance?

How can you purposefully cultivate greater emotional depth, transforming it into an invaluable asset in your leadership journey, thereby enhancing your ability to inspire and connect with those you lead?

> ### → Respond
>
> Practice journaling about your emotions using a color wheel to help you identify and categorize them. Take time to speak with those you love and trust: a spouse, partner, longtime friend, or a therapist or counselor. They will remind you that you are more than just your anger.

Day 31:
Facing Grief

It is better to go to the house of mourning than to go to the house of feasting.

—Ecclesiastes 7:2a

A LONG ROAD OF INFERTILITY HAS TESTED my marriage. Early in marriage my wife, Lindsey, wept, believing we'd never see the miracle we longed for—and to this day, still no miracle. For years I didn't allow myself to cry, but kept telling her to "have more faith." I suppressed my emotions by naively assuming everything would "work out" (meaning: getting pregnant and having a child), but this was just an unconscious strategy to sweep things under the rug. In so doing, I suppressed Lindsey's pain and dodged her emotions, I failed to offer the living presence of Jesus, and held fast to stoicism when I should have been sowing tears.

> Suppressed grief often turns into depression, anxiety, or addiction.
> –Miriam Greenspan[1]

Thankfully, we joined a small group of believers who felt stuck in various ways. During one of our sessions, the leader pointed his finger at me and sternly said, "David was a man who grieved and was called a man after God's own heart. You

---

1   Miriam Greenspan, *Healing Through the Dark Emotions: The Wisdom of Grief, Fear, and Despair* (Boston, MA: Shambhala, 2004), XII.

haven't done that." Those stern words shocked me out of passivity, and the next morning, as I sat reading the story of Lazarus, I finally broke open. Coming across the powerfully short line, "Jesus wept,"[2] I heard God tell me: "Lindsey's tears are My tears," and for the first time since we began our struggle, I wept too.

Embracing God's invitation to weep feels very counterintuitive doesn't it? As a Defender, you may say to yourself, "Sure, life can be hard, but why wallow in it?" Eights aren't the kind of people to sit around and feel sorry for themselves. But let me be blunt: Chances are, you've already endured loss or trauma by this point in your life. Can you say that you have properly grieved these experiences? Aside from life's accidents, your fearlessness often puts you on the front lines next to danger, leaving you even more susceptible to traumatic experiences. However, even in those times when you acknowledge the pain of abandonment, betrayal, or death—Eights often struggle with the fear of being "too much" for therapists or professionals to deal with, so you stay away.

Though it's easy to deny the pain, I want you to grasp the importance of embracing your grief—meaning acknowledging and processing it. Think of it as tending to a garden. All the unacknowledged hurt eventually takes root, becoming the unruly "weeds" that intermingle with the beautiful flowers and plants in your emotional landscape. If left unchecked, they can completely take over and prevent you from growing and thriving, which is why addressing and processing your grief is as vital as weeding a garden for its overall health, beauty, and fruitfulness.

> God has ordained that we set aside hours, days, or perhaps a season to mourn our losses.

One helpful passage for all Eights is Ecclesiastes 7:2, in which the Teacher reminds us, "It is better to go to the house of mourning than to go to the house of feasting." Earlier in chapter three, the Wise Sage explains that we should create space for both weeping and laughing, mourning and dancing.[3] Much like the

---

2   John 11:35

3   Ecclesiastes 3:4; We have much to learn from our Jewish brothers and sisters, who build periods of mourning into their lives, such as the practice of "sitting shiva" when someone in your community experiences loss.

Jewish calendar, which is full of times for both celebration and penance, God has ordained that we set aside hours, days, or perhaps a *season* to mourn our losses.

The Good News for Defenders is "The Lord is near to the brokenhearted and saves the crushed in spirit."[4] Underline the word "near" in that verse. When your heart gets broken or you are crushed, the Lord draws *near* to you. He will not tell you to pull yourself together but will always show up with His healing presence.

I recall a moment when my youngest son, Zeke, faced the hurtful rejection of a neighborhood friend. He sat on his bed, consumed by anger, pushing away any attempts at comfort. At that moment, I chose to sit at the end of his bed and stay with him until he finished venting and cursing. Then I gently helped him realize that beneath the anger was grief and behind the grief was an innocent love he felt for the friend he had lost.

Just as I sat with Zeke, the Father promises to sit with you in your grief. He wants to heal those emotional wounds that have been left unattended. Remember, those carrying hurt may perpetuate pain, but those who've been healed can bring strength and restoration to the world.

→ Pray

Father, give me the courage to grieve and lament, knowing it is a necessary part of healing and growth. Help me navigate my past with brutal honesty and vulnerability. Give me strength to draw near to others in their time of grief rather than distancing myself or offering emotional shortcuts.

---

[4] Psalm 34:18

Day 31 Reflections:

Where in your life might there be unresolved hurt or trauma? How can you begin to work through this grief with yourself, others, or a professional?

Ecclesiastes 7:2 encourages us to embrace both seasons of mourning and celebration. How can you proactively integrate moments for lamentation into your daily life?

Who currently needs your support in their time of loss or heartache, and how can you offer them your presence as they grieve?

> ### ➝ Respond
>
> Think about a painful experience and then write a prayer of lament using Psalm 22 as a guide. Express your grief over the loss of a loved one, personal failure or disappointments, unfulfilled dreams, childhood experiences, or social injustice.

Day 32:

It's Demo Day!

And the servants of the master of the house came and said to him, 'Master, did you not sow good seed in your field? How then does it have weeds?' He said to them, 'An enemy has done this.' So the servants said to him, 'Then do you want us to go and gather them?' But he said, 'No, lest in gathering the weeds you root up the wheat along with them.

—Matthew 13:27-29

WITH A DETERMINED GRIN, CHIP GAINES, HALF of the dynamic powerhouse duo behind the hit television show *Fixer Upper*, hollers these three words that never fail to spark excitement: "It's Demo Day!" As the walls crumble and the dust fills the air, there's an unmistakable energy—a sense of potential and transformation, of clearing away the unused or broken down to make way for something new. It's a moment of power and potential, echoing the essence of the Defender's spirit.

> The innate human capacity reflected in [Eight] nature is the energy of disruption.
> –Dr. Jerome D. Lubbe[1]

---

1 Jerome D. Lubbe, *The Brain-Based Enneagram: You are not A number* (Atlanta, GA: Thrive Neuro, 2020).

If Eights had a flag to represent their type, the central symbol would undoubtedly be a hammer: not only as a symbol of their willingness to "move fast and break things" but also as a declaration of their unyielding commitment to positive growth and change. These change makers don't fear disruption; they thrive in it. Just as Chip tears down walls to the studs, Eights have a natural inclination to determinedly dismantle barriers, apologetically challenge norms, and forge their own path. Jesus challenged the norms of the time, disrupting the status quo by confronting societal expectations, political power structures, and religious traditions. Yet we must remember that Christ sought to reform and rebuild without leaving a trail of destruction in His wake.

Unhealthy Eights, however, can be more *destructive* than *constructive*. In Matthew's Gospel, Jesus illustrated this truth in a parable in which a farmer sowed good seed in his field, only to have an enemy sneak in and sow weeds among his wheat. When the servants asked if they should uproot the weeds, the man responded with an unexpected answer: "Let both grow together until the harvest."[2] This wise farmer knows disrupting the soil will not only destroy the weeds but also the wheat, completely ruining any chance at a good harvest.

> **Disrupting the soil will not only destroy the weeds but the wheat.**

This is a powerful lesson for Eights who desire change but often seek it without considering the collateral damage. Your natural capacity for disruption will leave you ecstatic at the thought of bringing in the wrecking ball, but others may feel like your disruptive methods are a threat to their current peace and security.

While some matters, such as the justice of righting historic societal wrongs, require a fearless disruptor, other areas require much more *finesse*. The workplace, for example, will often find the average to unhealthy Eight implementing an entirely new organizational structure without proper consultation or preparation, leading to confusion and resistance. They may replace key team members without a comprehensive succession plan, or overhaul the group's mission or metrics, all

---

2 Matthew 13:30

of which lead to resentment or decreased employee engagement and, ultimately, lowered effectiveness.

I'm not saying you should stop using your superpower of cultivating growth but to give yourself a little more time, so you don't uproot the trust of your most loyal followers. Remember, God allows the good and the bad to coexist for a season so that transformation can take its course without too many unnecessary interventions or destruction of the whole system.

The Good News for Defenders is that when the time for harvest arrives, the yield will be so abundant that there will be a shortage of workers to gather it all in![3] If you resist the temptation of an instant reward through destruction and rely on the Holy Spirit for more patience, then you'll reap a greater reward later.[4]

Here are some practical sowing strategies which, while focused on the workplace, have analogues to our daily relationships: Take more time to understand the existing dynamics better; communicate transparently to build trust; identify specific areas for incremental change; engage key stakeholders in the decision-making process; and conduct pilot programs for testing. Incorporating these strategies ensures smoother transitions and greater acceptance of changes.

Take a cue from Chip and Joanna Gaines, who constructively reuse materials in every home they renovate. Though it takes more time, their deliberate preservation of existing hardwood floors, ceiling fixtures, and timeless pieces not only retains the original charm but also elevates the property's value. Similarly, if you go about seeking renovation with more discernment, you can safeguard the invaluable assets that make up the current foundation of your group, relationships, and yourself, maintaining a strong connection to history while paving the way for a more vibrant future.

---

3   Luke 10:2

4   Galatians 5:22-23

→ Pray

Father, thank You for sending Your Son, Jesus, to be a model of a healthy change agent. Help me by the Spirit's power to wield my strength not as a wrecking ball but as an instrument of mindful progress. May my actions be rooted in a spirit of understanding and patience, recognizing that true transformation requires time and discernment.

Day 32 Reflections:

How has God used your natural capacity for disruption to be instrumental in challenging established norms and promoting positive change?

Consider when you may have acted hastily in making changes without fully assessing the potential consequences. How did this impact your relationships and the overall environment?

What strategies mentioned can you employ to deliberately approach change, foster smoother transitions, and garner greater acceptance for your proposed changes?

→ Respond

Engage key partners or stakeholders today in discussions about potential modifications to a plan or project, encouraging their valuable input and feedback.

Day 33:

BS Detector

Nathan said to David, "You are the man! Thus says the L<small>ORD</small>*, the God of Israel, 'I anointed you king over Israel, and I delivered you out of the hand of Saul. And I gave you your master's house and your master's wives into your arms and gave you the house of Israel and of Judah. And if this were too little, I would add to you as much more. Why have you despised the word of the* L<small>ORD</small>*, to do what is evil in his sight?*

—2 Samuel 12:7-9a

A<small>LL</small> E<small>IGHTS</small> <small>HAVE</small> <small>A</small> <small>BUILT-IN</small> BS <small>DETECTOR</small>. They carry their own mental polygraph machine with them wherever they go because they simply want the truth, the whole truth, and nothing but the truth. Possessing an innate ability to perceive falsehoods and deceptions, their powerful internal radar cuts through facades, revealing the unvarnished truth hidden beneath layers of pretense. They know how to "apply just the right amount of pressure for the real person behind the mask

> But better to get hurt by the truth than be comforted with a lie.
>
> –Khaled Hosseini[1]

---

1 Khaled Hosseini, *The Kite Runner: Rejacketed* (India: Bloomsbury, 2011), 50.

Day 33

to pop out,"[2] which is why Ian Cron humorously warns others, "If [Eights] trust you, you've got it made. If they don't, sleep with one eye open."[3]

The author of Hebrews likens truth to a double-edged sword, "piercing to the division of soul and of spirit, of joints and marrow, and discerning the thoughts and intentions of the heart."[4] In other words, God's Living Word cuts through the mess and brings to light hidden intentions, agendas, and hypocrisy. The apostle Paul adds that Scripture is useful for "reproof,"[5] a word which means to test someone to expose their true nature and hold them accountable for wrongdoing.[6]

Eights are the church's modern-day prophets, whom God has appointed to sternly convey His truth, call for repentance, advocate for social justice but also graciously offer hope and encouragement to the church, promising God's faithfulness and restoration if they return to Him in obedience. A prophet's job is much less about *foretelling* than it is about *forthtelling*—speaking truth to power and caring enough to challenge the bullies of the world, oftentimes being the first to call out the wolves in sheep's clothing.[7] That's why Alison Hamm jokingly told me, "As an Eight, I've often said I am the middle finger of the body of Christ."

> All Eights have a built-in BS detector.

The act of *confronting* someone or a group of people is critical because there can be no true justice without confrontation. As Henry Nouwen eloquently explained, "We cannot suffer with the poor when we are unwilling to confront those persons and systems that cause poverty. We cannot set the captives free when we do not want to confront those who carry the keys. We cannot profess our solidarity with those who are oppressed when we are unwilling to confront the oppressor. Compassion without confrontation fades quickly to fruitless sentimental commiseration."[8]

---

2 Wagner, *Nine Lenses on the World*, 409.
3 Cron and Stabile, *The Road Back to You*, 56-57.
4 Hebrews 4:12
5 2 Timothy 3:16
6 H. Cariss J. Sidnell. "Reproof - Hastings' Dictionary of the New Testament." StudyLight.org. Accessed November 9, 2023. https://www.studylight.org/dictionaries/eng/hdn/r/reproof.html.
7 Matthew 7:15
8 Stabile, *The Journey Toward Wholeness*, 195.

For instance, when God sent Nathan to confront King David, we find a man who believed he had used his power to successfully steal another man's wife, get her pregnant, and then kill him to destroy the evidence. But the prophet Nathan, compelled by God, approached David with a parable about a rich man who unjustly took a poor man's only beloved lamb. As David reacted with anger, declaring that the rich man deserved to die, Nathan dropped the punch line: *You are that man.* He then rebuked David, exposing his heinous actions and prophesying the consequences that would follow.[9] Nathan's confrontation shows us that out of God's great compassion for victims of injustice, He will not stop until the Uriahs of the world are avenged.

The Good News for Defenders is Jesus came as a prophet to bring justice to the world and gives you permission to do the same. Lean into your role as "challenger" without apology. Remember that as an Eight, your unique ability to *forthtell*—to debunk falsehoods and expose the truth—is a gift given to you by God. Just as Nathan fearlessly confronted the powerful King David, know that your role as a modern-day prophet is essential for upholding righteousness in the world.

When the time comes to confront, make a plan first—like Jesus did when He went into the temple with His makeshift whip of chords. Make no mistake: He did not fly off the handle in anger as some have said but executed a pre-planned act to make a prophetic point. Similarly, when you feel compelled to confront, plan strategically, choose the right setting, maintain composure, and offer the wrongdoer a clear path toward repentance, reconciliation, and restitution. And as you walk in the footsteps of Nathan and Christ Himself, the ultimate truth-telling Living Word, remember that you are a powerful reflection of God's enduring compassion for all His people.

→ Pray

Father, thank You for giving us Your truth, a double-edged sword, to cut through the layers of deceit and hypocrisy, revealing the intentions and motives of our hearts. Give me the ability to confront wrongdoing in a manner that reflects Your grace and love. In all that I do, may Your enduring compassion for all people shine through.

---

9 2 Samuel 12:1-12

Day 33 Reflections:

Can you recall a time when your BS detector or readiness to confront has positively influenced your community, workplace, or relationships?

Reflecting on occasions when you were confronted by others, how have you typically responded? How open have you been to receiving corrections and feedback?

What steps can you take to ensure your confrontations are well-planned and intended to foster repentance and reconciliation?

→ Respond

Approach an individual or group who needs to be confronted in a private and respectful setting and initiate a dialogue that is focused on understanding and resolution rather than on blame or accusation.

Day 34:

The Illusion of Invincibility

The LORD is my rock and my fortress and my deliverer, my God, my rock, in whom I take refuge, my shield, and the horn of my salvation, my stronghold.

—Psalm 18:2

BEKAH WAS TOTALLY INTO SUPERHEROES AS A kid. She'd spend hours reading comic books, picturing herself as this awesome hero, saving people and fighting the bad guys. As Bekah started high school, she hit the gym hard, aiming to be the toughest kid in school, and quickly came to realize that others seemed to respect her more when she didn't complain, show much emotion, or have a lot of needs.

> It is better to die on your feet than to live on your knees.
> –Emiliano Zapata

However, after graduation and the onset of the "real world," the pressures of trying to be a bulletproof hero started getting to her. Eventually, after pushing herself harder and harder without taking any time off, it all got to be too much. Bekah, who used to be so full of energy, started burning out. One night, feeling exhausted and physically sick, she came to the realization that the idea of becoming invincible like Wonder Woman, while inspiring in fictional stories, wasn't sustainable in real life.

Day 34

The feeling of invincibility for an average Eight may manifest as feeling "physically bigger and more powerful than they are, so they'll place unreasonable demands on their bodies and put their health and well-being at risk."[1] For unhealthy Eights, this may mean ignoring the warnings about things like over-exertion, bad eating habits, or harmful substances. The unconscious thought is "It won't happen to me. I'm too strong to be affected by this stuff."[2]

It's only when we realize that *living without limits is what's limiting you* that we can begin to grow beyond our self-sufficiency complex. God wants you to stay in your lane and observe the rules of human nature like the rest of us so that you can finish the race strong. That begins with redefining rest as *renewal* rather than *weakness*. All quality health professionals and trainers will tell you that the time of *rest* following a workout is just as vital as the time spent on the bench. After going to the gym and pushing yourself, overcoming all of those obstacles of resistance called weights, science has shown that your muscles literally tear apart. But for those muscles to heal, double in size, and make you stronger, a rhythm of rest is required. Going fast and furious will only weaken you, making all your good effort counterproductive.

> **Living without limits is what's limiting you.**

When average Eights burn out, they move to the low side of Type Five, isolating themselves by cutting off communication with those who love and support them. Typically, they will then either beat up on themselves for being weak or gather ammunition so that they can plot revenge. Unhealthy Eights may implode, refusing support or comfort and driving themselves into a black hole while the gravitational force of their personality pulls everyone into that silence with them.[3]

Healthy Eights, however, move to the high side of Type Five under stress and learn how to set healthy boundaries, say no more, learn to enjoy time alone, become more introspective, devote themselves to learning and personal passions, and take the time to analyze different perspectives and options.

---

1 Cron and Stabile, *The Road Back to You*, 54.
2 Riso and Hudson, *The Wisdom of the Enneagram*, 299.
3 Wagner, *Nine Lenses on the World*, 430.

The Good News for Defenders is you can take off the cape because we already have a Superhero. As King David sang, God is our Rock, Deliverer, Refuge, Shield, Salvation, and Stronghold.[4] Knowing that Jesus has a cape and you do not does not make you less strong. After all, Jesus gave His disciple Simon a new name: Peter, which means "rock"[5] and entrusted him with the keys to become the de facto leader of the first century church! You are our "Peter," the one we can rely on to help us follow Jesus courageously and prevail over the gates of hell.[6]

Like Peter after his personal transformation, when you lead with *vulnerability*, you point others to God's *invincibility*. This means taking off your cape more often and depending on others more; by asking for help instead of always having to be everyone else's rock. Becoming completely dependent on others may feel very awkward at first, but the restorative effect that others' strengths will have on you will eventually feel reinvigorating.

→ **Pray**

Father, show me that true strength isn't about pretending to be invincible but about recognizing my limits and allowing myself the rest I need to recover. Teach me to be open to support, to see my own limits and set boundaries, and to let others in, knowing that I don't have to face my battles alone. I will embrace my human side today while leaning on You as my Rock of Salvation.

---

[4] Psalm 18:2

[5] Mikeal C. Parsons. "Peter - Holman Bible Dictionary." StudyLight.org. Accessed November 9, 2023. https://www.studylight.org/dictionaries/hbd/p/peter.html.

[6] Matthew 16:18

Day 34 Reflections:

Recall a time when you pushed yourself too hard and experienced burnout. How did you handle it, and what insights did you gain from that experience?

_____
_____
_____
_____

How can you practically embody the concept of "taking off the cape" in your life? In what ways can you allow yourself to be more vulnerable and less invincible?

_____
_____
_____
_____

Where in your current schedule can you integrate new rhythms of rest? What boundaries do you need to establish to prioritize self-care?

_____
_____
_____
_____

> ### → Respond
>
> Select a specific date and time within the next six weeks for intentional rest. Block off this time in your calendar as non-negotiable, treating it as you would any other crucial appointment or commitment.

Day 35:
Rising Above Revenge

Repay no one evil for evil, but give thought to do what is honorable in the sight of all. If possible, so far as it depends on you, live peaceably with all. Beloved, never avenge yourselves, but leave it to the wrath of God, for it is written, "Vengeance is mine, I will repay, says the Lord."

—Romans 12:17-19

SOME OF MY FAVORITE STORIES AND MOVIES are about vigilantes—those who won't take no for an answer when it comes to dishing out justice. All too often, though, these fighters' ideas of payback can get a little sketchy (and bloody)! Are they balancing the scales, or just adding more weight to the chaos? Has their pursuit of justice led them to become anti-heroes or even villains?

> Man must evolve for all human conflict a method which rejects revenge, aggression, and retaliation. The foundation of such a method is love.
> –Martin Luther King Jr.[1]

As a Defender, you have that same fire in your belly, that burning desire to make things

---

[1] Riso and Hudson, *The Wisdom of the Enneagram*, 286.

right, as all the great masked heroes and caped crusaders do. Eights are not vindictive—they just don't want to feel abused or taken advantage of. However, one of the common lies Eights are tempted to believe is that forgiveness or compromise invites further abuse.[2] They come to believe *revenge works*, which is why Oscar Ichazo, the creator of the modern Enneagram, taught that an Eight's fixation is *vengeance*.[3]

When unhealthy, Eights will spend a lot of time contemplating revenge scenarios in their heads to "get even" with the people who've hurt or betrayed them. After all, they must be the ones to deliver justice and right all the wrongs they see in the world, because if they don't, who will?[4] This logic makes perfect sense in a world where God doesn't exist, and cries for justice disappear into the empty heavens. This leaves every Eight with a vital question: *Do I truly believe God can see all and that He will one day right the wrongs of the world?*

One day Jesus sent out His disciples ahead of Him to go into a Samaritan village, but the people did not welcome Him there. When the disciples James and John saw this, they angrily asked, "Lord, do you want us to call fire down from heaven to destroy them?"[5] It seems a bit excessive to most modern ears, but it is a legitimate question. Shouldn't those standing in the way of our Savior be punished? As a side note, I want to point out the fact that it's much easier to "call down fire" on someone when they are the *other* and when you think Jesus is on your side. Just think about how much vengeance has been done in the name of God throughout history.

> **You can get on with your life without getting even.**

Eights can stay off this path of vengeance by paying close attention to any ways they may be rationalizing their fiery words and actions toward their enemies *or* friends. Richard Rohr commented that the root sin of an Eight is *shamelessness*, which means they have the capacity to live unashamed of the ways they treat

---

2 Palmer, *The Enneagram in Love and Work*, 208.
3 Chestnut, *The Complete Enneagram*.
4 Chestnut and Paes, *The Enneagram Guide to Waking Up*, 210.
5 Luke 9:54 NIV

others when they think they're right.[6] To give an example, a pastor I knew once pointed out to a fellow Eight pastor, "The problem is not that you are wrong. It's just that you are being an ass."

The Good News for Defenders is that God truly is in control, never forgets an injustice, and defends you against your enemies. He has not forgotten the loud cries of every ancient martyr and modern-day victim who pleads, "O Sovereign Lord, holy and true, how long before you will judge and avenge our blood on those who dwell on the earth?"[7] Take comfort in His response: "[Just] wait a little longer."[8]

The apostle Paul warns us to not avenge ourselves because revenge *doesn't work*. It wastes a significant amount of your emotional and mental energy, does not address the root causes of the issue, does not seek a true resolution, and keeps you stuck in the past rather than moving toward the future. And ultimately, it displays a lack of faith in God's vision, wisdom, and timing.

Leaving our enemies in God's hands is the only way to prevent a continuous cycle of hostility and violence in the world and instead move us toward reconciliation and understanding, like Jesus who "continued entrusting himself to him who judges justly."[9] In this surrender, you'll find a peace that surpasses all understanding—one that allows you to finally realize that you can get on with your life without getting even.

→ Pray

Father, guide me to release the weight of past wrongs and the thoughts of retribution that consume me. Teach me the power of forgiveness and the healing it brings. Give me the strength to resist using Your name to justify actions that don't reflect Your true nature.

---

6   Rohr and Ebert, *The Enneagram*, 168.

7   Revelation 6:10

8   Revelation 6:11 NIV

9   1 Peter 2:23

Day 35 Reflections:

Have you ever asked God to metaphorically (or literally!) "call down fire" on someone for acting unjustly? Consider how events might have unfolded differently if your request had been granted.[10]

When has your strong sense of righteousness led you to treat others unrighteously?

What is the difference between seeking justice and vengeance? How does vengeance distort our perspective on resolving conflicts?

→ Respond

Listen to Bob Dylan's classic "With God On Our Side" and consider how rationalizing our actions becomes easier when we feel God is for us and against our *other*.

---

10 Calhoun and Loughrige, *Spiritual Rhythms*, 23.

Day 36:

No Mercy

For judgment is without mercy to one who has shown

no mercy. Mercy triumphs over judgment.

—James 2:13

IN THE CLASSIC MOVIE *THE KARATE KID*, Cobra Kai is the infamous karate school known for its aggressive and merciless approach to martial arts. Their slogan, "Strike first, strike hard, no mercy,"[2] flows from the belief that mercy is a sign of weakness that only allows your adversaries to exploit you. Winning leaves no room for compassion or the smallest amount of leniency.

> **Strike first, strike hard, no mercy,**
> –Cobra Kai's slogan, The Karate Kid[1]

Though some Defenders may resemble the Cobra Kai approach to life, the truth is that all Eights are first and foremost merciless toward *themselves*. Meredith Boggs shares from personal experience, "When emotionally checked in and self aware, [Eights] can see the magnitude of the hurt their

---

1 "The Karate Kid." IMDb. Accessed November 9, 2023. https://www.imdb.com/title/tt0087538/characters/nm0184392.

2 Ibid.

actions and anger can cause. They may seem unfazed, but internally they are berating themselves and beating themselves up."[3]

God's invitation to Eights is to both give and *receive* mercy,[4] which is no small task for those who hold justice in such high regard. After their banishment from Eden, Adam and Eve had two sons, named Cain and Abel. While still young men, both sons made an offering to God, yet it was the younger, Abel, whose offering was accepted, while Cain's was rejected. Fueled by jealousy and anger, Cain killed his brother in cold blood. When confronted by God, Cain denied both his actions and his responsibility to his brother, leading God to say, "What have you done? The voice of your brother's blood is crying to me from the ground."[5]

The author of Hebrews, looking back on this story through the lens of Christ, poetically said the blood of Jesus "speaks a better word than the blood of Abel."[6] While the blood of Abel cried for *justice* against the one man who wronged him, the blood of Jesus cries *mercy—mercy for all people, from Cain up to you and me*. Abel's murder became a protest for retribution, but Jesus' murder became a proclamation of grace.

> **Abel's murder became a protest for retribution, but Jesus' murder became a proclamation of grace.**

Like Cain, many of us have "blood on our hands" over the divisiveness we've sown and people we've hurt. And, while the strong voice inside your own head would like to put you on the stand, point the finger, and demand retribution, the blood of Jesus cries out *mercy* over your soul from the empty tomb. When overwhelming and paralyzing feelings of guilt flood your heart over your past, God only has only one word to say to you: *mercy*.

Jesus' blood has something to say to your enemies too. You may have been accused, attacked, abused, oppressed, shamed, insulted, or rejected by a "Cain" in your life. So let me ask you: Who are your Cains? Who do you need to

---

3   Boggs, *The Journey Home*, 46.
4   Rohr and Ebert, *The Enneagram*, 176.
5   Genesis 4:10
6   Hebrews 12:24

speak Christ's "better word" over? Who do you need to declare "mercy" over in your prayers?

Remember, forgiveness is not a sign of weakness but strength. Nor does it imply that justice should or will be discarded altogether. Rather, it is a powerful choice to release you from the burden of bitterness. It allows you to break free from the chains of anger that can bind you for years or even decades. In choosing forgiveness, you reclaim your spiritual power, refusing to let past hurts dictate your present and future.

The bad news according to James the brother of Jesus, is "There will be no mercy for those who have not shown mercy to others."[7] In other words, to the extent we demand punishment, punishment will be given to us. But . . .

The Good News for Defenders is that in God's eyes, "Mercy triumphs over judgment."[8] The currency of God's economy is mercy. Remember, it was God's *hesed*—His *loving-kindness*—that led us to repentance rather than the merciless Cobra Kais of the world.[9] God did not win us to His team through condemnation or guilt trips but through a merciful and forgiving embrace. Treat others with the same compassion and understanding, so God might use your kindness to pave the way for your enemies to choose their own new story of hope and grace.

→ Pray

Father, sometimes I've let a harsh attitude rule, both toward myself and others, neglecting the power of mercy. Help me break free from guilt and self-condemnation and extend forgiveness to myself and those I've seen as adversaries. Remind me that in Your Kingdom, mercy triumphs over judgment.

---

7   James 2:13 NLT

8   James 2:13

9   Romans 2:4

Day 36 Reflections:

Where in your life are you still prone to feeling guilt or self-condemnation? In which areas do you long to hear God's voice speaking mercy into your soul?

Who in your life has exhibited behavior like Cain's? How can you strive to offer them mercy and forgiveness, promoting the journey of healing and reconciliation?

In what aspects of your life have you observed the impact of a "Cobra Kai" mindset? How can you create space for mercy, recognizing it as a display of strength rather than weakness?

> ### → Respond
>
> Write a forgiveness letter to someone you hold resentment toward and honestly express your feelings. Include a statement entrusting the situation to God, releasing the need for retribution and acknowledging that justice lies in His hands.

Day 37:

Mafia Leaders

I will surely bless you, and I will surely multiply your offspring as the stars of heaven and as the sand that is on the seashore. And your offspring shall possess the gate of his enemies, and in your offspring shall all the nations of the earth be blessed, because you have obeyed my voice.

—Genesis 22:17-18

IN ALL MAFIA STORIES, AMID THE SUSPENSEFUL plots and high-stakes drama, one powerful theme consistently emerges: the unyielding love for and fierce protection of the family at all costs. From the Godfather's unwavering commitment to his kin, to Tony Soprano's balancing of familial love and commitment to the larger "family," the essence of family and its preservation stands at the heart of these compelling narratives.

> The strength of a family, like the strength of an army, lies in its loyalty to each other.
> —Don Vito Corleone, The Godfather[1]

I always joke that Defenders would make great mafia leaders because their top priority is to safeguard the family—they

---

1 Parade. "Luca Brasi Sleeps With the Fishes!" 60 Memorable Quotes From The Godfather. Accessed November 9, 2023. https://parade.com/1337760/parade/godfather-quotes/.

Day 37

will do whatever is necessary to ensure their well-being and safety. *La famiglia* is not an afterthought but the first thought. Because of this mindset, Eights make incredible parents, caregivers, mentors, and compassionate leaders.

Healthy Eights are warm and generous parents who excel at empowering their children, especially the less-assured ones. In fact, Eights strive to teach all of their loved ones how to advocate and care for themselves. Riso and Hudson comment that Eights are good at building up the strength of their children, much like a protective "lioness nudging her cubs along or teaching them the ways of nature."[2] Author Jacqui Pollock teaches that healthy Eights raise their children in an environment of security and love, and their sheer fun and energetic spirit along with their *joie de vivre* makes life contagious. Because Eights are courageous and resourceful, they lead their family members to try new, fun, and adventurous opportunities that other families may miss out on. Additionally, an Eight's strong sense of justice empowers those under their care to stand up for what's right no matter the cost.[3]

> Eights are warm and generous parents who excel at empowering their children.

On the flip side, Pollock explains that unhealthy Eights may become distant or remote when they get stressed or push themselves to the point of exhaustion. They pile on the pressure, often leading to an explosion, or they become restless and impatient when loved ones "just don't get it." Children can become overwhelmed or frightened when the Eight's anger comes out. When Eights are at their least healthy, tendencies toward being controlling and even manipulative may come out when the child doesn't follow the rules or do what you say. However, it's imperative for the family to understand that an Eight's strength and assertiveness can easily be misconstrued as aggression.[4]

On the bright side, healthy Eights keep pushing themselves to grow in creating space for their children and partner, fostering an environment where everyone's voices are heard. They ask thoughtful questions, allowing for independent thought

---

2   Riso and Hudson, *Personality Types*, 311.

3   Ibid, 141-143.

4   Ibid, 143-144.

to nurture their children's unique personalities and build a sense of autonomy. They balance their protective instincts and keep from becoming controlling. They become more considerate and less blunt in their communication to foster a more nurturing atmosphere. They slow down to consider others' perspectives and openly express when they feel worried, anxious, or sad to build an empathetic family dynamic.[5]

The Good News for Defenders is God empowers you to use your innate protective strengths while freeing you from the fear, violence, intimidation, and legal consequences associated with running a Mafia family!

With Eight-like faith and courage, the patriarchs of God's original *famiglia*, Abraham and Sarah, left their comfortable homeland in the Fertile Crescent and embarked on a journey to the land of Canaan. They navigated various challenges and trials, like famine, family conflicts, infertility, regional politics, and much more. Though Abraham and Sarah were far from perfect, it would be these two ordinary individuals from whom God would create an extraordinary family, with "descendants as numerous as the stars."[6]

Similar to Abraham and Sarah, you may not know exactly where God is leading you next. You may feel like a stranger in a strange land, but one thing remains clear: If you have become part of Abraham and Sarah's spiritual lineage, you haven't just received God's blessings but a call to serve in the line of patriarchs and matriarchs. God is counting on you to uphold the legacy of faith and set a compelling example for the generations to come. Through your life, God intends to expand His ethnically diverse family, embracing every neighborhood, nation, and culture on earth.

→ Pray

Father, thank You for giving me such a strong commitment to my family. Help me remember that You know what's best for them. Loosen my grip so I won't get in the way of all my loved ones being used mightily for Your purposes. I will surrender all of my fears to You today regarding my family.

---

5   Ibid, 149-150.

6   Genesis 22:17 NIV

Day 37 Reflections:

How have your protective strengths positively influenced your family?

In what ways have you seen your intensity, anger, or controlling tendencies negatively affect your family?

What aspects of assuming the responsibility of a patriarch or matriarch in God's family ignite your enthusiasm?

> ### → Respond
>
> Create an "I Surrender" list, and name all the anxieties you can think of regarding one family member: a wandering faith, unhealthy habits, toxic friendships, and so on. Entrust that individual to God, mirroring the act of surrender Abraham was asked to demonstrate with his son, Isaac.

Day 38:

Trust Issues

In God I trust; I shall not be afraid. What can man do to me?

—Psalm 56:11

ON A VACATION TO SAN FRANCISCO, MY wife and I hopped in a rental car and traveled north to Muir Woods, a large redwood forest where some of the trees reach 250 feet high and 30 feet in diameter! As I stood under their breathtaking enormity, I considered how many of these millennia-old trees were just sprouting seeds when Jesus walked the earth. Can you imagine how much wind, rain, and lightning these trees have battled over the past two thousand years? Talk about resiliency!

Like these redwoods, you have the strength and potential to grow into something truly magnificent. You were not created to be a small house plant but a great tree that can weather endless storms. But, as with all plants, there's a catch: For a seed to become a tree, it first has to die by going into the ground and shedding its protective coat. You, too, must shed that tough

> The life's work of the Eight is learning to trust.
> –Meredith Boggs[1]

---

1 Boggs, *The Journey Home*, 38.

shell and let others in if you want to draw strength from the life-giving water and nurturing soil of your community.

Your great challenge as a Defender will be to learn how to trust others daily. Famously, redwoods do not have deep roots; rather than extending deep underground, they grow outward, intermingling with the rest of the forest, each strengthening the next. You too have to resist that urge to live independently from the forest. Like the redwoods, you must send your roots out, opening yourself to vulnerable connections—to both joy and pain.

It's no secret that many Eights have trust issues; it takes a long time to trust people, especially if they have experienced betrayals. After everything King David had to go through, he had trust issues too, which is why he penned the words, "It is better to take refuge in the Lord than to trust in humans."[2] He knew that even the most seasoned believers can surprise us with shocking immaturity. As Meredith Boggs writes, "The life's work of the Eight is learning to trust."[3] Trust will never be something that you can conquer or check off a list; it's a growth path you'll have to walk your whole life.

> Your great challenge as a Defender will be to learn how to trust others daily.

Just as God tested Abraham in asking him to sacrifice his son, Isaac, to find out what was really in his heart, Eights also tend to test others, although this strategy is often unconscious. They test by challenging authority, aiming to gauge the reliability of a leader's character or plans. They push boundaries to determine whether others possess the fortitude necessary to confront difficult situations or hold their ground. They keenly observe others' responses to conflicts, evaluating their trustworthiness when pressured. Lastly, they may test the loyalty of others, striving to ascertain whether others are dependable enough to remain steadfast and committed at their side.

The only problem is that the rest of us don't always pick up on what you are doing, so your growth path is to learn to recognize when you activate this "test"

---

2 Psalm 118:8 NIV

3 Boggs, *The Journey Home*, 38.

mode, to communicate openly and honestly, and to be understanding with others' misunderstandings and even defensiveness.

The Good News for Defenders is as David said: "In God I trust; I shall not be afraid. What can man do to me?"[4] Fearing what man *could* do to you may lead to constantly anticipating betrayal, becoming overly protective, testing others to the point of exhaustion, or avoiding relational commitment altogether and ultimately ending up alone. But nurturing your trust in God allows you to trade control for inner peace, find rest for your mind and body, and even learn to trust your all-too-human loved ones and partners.

Just as young David faced betrayal from King Saul, he nevertheless fostered a profound friendship with the king's son Jonathan—one characterized by unwavering loyalty and genuine love. God desires to bless you with such companions as well. Regardless of past experiences, God wants to give you more "Jonathans" who are eager to offer their wholehearted support, even sometimes at great personal cost. Such is your ability to inspire strength and love in those around you—if you are willing to let them in.

→ Pray

Father, open my eyes to the barriers that obstruct my ability to trust and help me to communicate openly with others about my struggle. Bless me with loyal friendships that mirror the profound bond shared by David and Jonathan and allow others to witness the beauty that emerges when we dare to embrace vulnerability and take risks in trust.

---

4   Psalm 56:11

Day 38 Reflections:

What is one specific protective shell or barrier that you recognize is hindering your ability to trust and form deep connections with others?

Can you identify ways you might be unintentionally testing others? How might this be impacting your relationships, and how can you work to improve this dynamic?

Though past experiences that may have influenced your trust in others, how can you cultivate deep and meaningful friendships similar to David and Jonathan's?

→ Respond

Rather than punishing or cutting someone off after they've breached your trust, try setting and communicating the right expectations as well as boundaries for future interactions, providing the opportunity for the relationship to be rebuilt.

Day 39:

Making the Impossible Possible

With man this is impossible, but with God all things are possible.

—Matthew 19:26

On August 30, 2023, the Nebraska Cornhusker volleyball team made history in a groundbreaking match at Memorial Football Stadium. Initially aiming to surpass the 18,755 attendance record set by the Wisconsin Badgers in 2021, their soaring ticket sales prompted them to dream even higher. The previous US attendance record for a women's sporting event stood at 90,185, during the 1999 World Cup, and the world record was just beyond this, at 91,648 in Barcelona, Spain.[2]

> Only those who will risk going too far can possibly find out how far one can go.
>
> –T.S. Eliot[1]

A day before this momentous event, junior setter Kennedi Orr distributed a letter to each team member and staff, with Coach John Cook reciting a poignant line: "Tomorrow, we

---

1 Elizabeth Wagele, *The Enneagram for Teens: Discover Your Personality Type and Celebrate Your True Self* (United States: PLI MEDIA, 2014).

2 Michael Voepel. "Nebraska Volleyball Sets World Record for Women's Sports Attendance." ESPN. Accessed November 9, 2023. https://www.espn.com/college-sports/story/_/id/38294591/nebraska-volleyball-sets-world-record-attendance-women-sporting-event.

make the impossible possible." On the night of the match, the team entered the stadium through the tunnel with fog and lights to the resounding cheers of an unprecedented 92,003 fans. They had just set a new national *and* world attendance record, leaving an enduring legacy in the realm of women's athletics.³

Defenders have the mustard seed of faith that can move mountains. They don't dwell on what's possible but seek to achieve the impossible. Healthy Eights seem to part one Red Sea after another with God's staff in hand, causing the rest of us to shake our heads in disbelief and wonder. They are visionary leaders driven by an unwavering self-confidence, willpower, and a can-do attitude that seems to gain energy when they are challenged or doubted. As Jane Austen said in *Pride and Prejudice*, "There is a stubbornness about me that never can bear to be frightened at the will of others. My courage always rises with every attempt to intimidate me."⁴

Fearlessness is at the core of an Eight's character. You stand up to bullies and pursue impossible dreams, even if they aren't easy. Your resilience and boldness, paired with an ambitious and strategic mindset, enables you to master the art of seeing potential where others only see scraps; to take calculated risks; and to seize opportunities for success. Are there no resources for the vision? No problem. Like Jesus, you can take what's in a little boy's lunch box and trust God to miraculously multiply it to exponential proportions.⁵ Your off-the-charts confidence also gives the power to rally others to build something monumental, confront systemic issues, or forge paths and partnerships where none seemed to exist before.

> Defenders have the mustard seed of faith that can move mountains.

After wandering around the desert for forty years, the Israelites started to believe the Promised Land was a pipe dream. After being tasked with scouting the land of Canaan, most of the returning spies were overwhelmed by the sight of giants and succumbed to fear, casting doubt on the possibility of inheriting their

---

3   "Making the Impossible Possible." University of Nebraska - Official Athletics Website. Accessed November 9, 2023. https://huskers.com/news/2023/09/12/making-the-impossible-possible.

4   Jane Austen, *Pride and Prejudice* (New York, NY: Penguin Group Inc., 2008), 170.

5   Matthew 14:16-18

dreamland. But Joshua and Caleb, with an Eight-like conquering spirit, exhorted them to march forward after God clearly told them, "Have I not commanded you? Be strong and courageous. Do not be frightened, and do not be dismayed, for the Lord your God is with you wherever you go."[6]

You also must heed God's call, embracing your gift of bringing *this* generation to the promised land, tirelessly working to turn that vision into a tangible reality, no matter the obstacles. If this call remains answered, the church risks wandering aimlessly for another period of testing. It is crucial for you to use your fearlessness to help us conquer the spiritual strongholds and giants of our time and to expand the Kingdom's reach, enabling us to venture deeper into enemy territory and claim what has always been rightfully ours.

The Good News for Defenders is that "in all these things we are more than conquerors through him who loved us."[7] I understand that while *you* may hold to this truth, not everyone does. It can be daunting to confront the overwhelming giants of political polarization, injustice and inequality, global conflicts and warfare, environmental degradation, ethical decline, and an increasingly nihilistic worldview. However, God has assured us that just beyond these challenges lies a realm of peace, joy, unity, love, restoration, abundance, and beauty. So, continue to inspire us with your compelling visions, reminding us that while faith may not make things easy, it can always make them possible.

→ Pray

Father, in the face of adversity and doubt, help me to hold onto Your promise that I am more than a conqueror. Help me lead the church toward a brighter future. Let my bold faith be a testament to others of Your unwavering love and power, and may my life reflect the fearlessness that comes from trusting in You.

---

[6] Joshua 1:9

[7] Romans 8:37

Day 39 Reflections:

Reflect on a time when you faced a seemingly insurmountable challenge. How did your fearlessness and unwavering self-confidence guide you through that situation?

How can you use your visionary leadership to inspire others to pursue their dreams, no matter how impossible they seem?

Identify the major obstacles or "giants" of this generation. How can you inspire others to have faith and overcome these challenges?

→ Respond

Create a "trophy case" by making a list of your past successes.[8] Just as rubble from the walls of Jericho gave the Israelites confidence as they marched on to conquer bigger cities, use your trophy case to give you confidence to take on greater challenges.

---

8 Moser, *The Enneagram of Discernment*, 184.

Day 40:
Eightness Is Greatness

Truly, I say to you, among those born of women there has arisen no one greater than John the Baptist.

—Matthew 11:11a

PROPHESIED ONE. PROPHET. LEADER. ZEALOT. DEMON-POSSESSED. JOHN the Baptist had many epithets, and even more mystery surrounding his identity and his role in God's plan. Yet wherever this charismatic, weirdo preacher went—even the middle of the desert—crowds followed him, listening to his fiery calls for repentance and submitting to baptism in the River Jordan. John's fearless critique of all ungodly leaders led him to confront King Herod Antipas, who married his brother's wife, Herodias; a battle that would eventually and tragically lead to his grisly execution.

> He who is brave is free.
> –Lucius Annaeus Seneca

Defenders will find a lot of similarities between their stories and John's. Eights are often known for their fearlessness in confronting injustice, calling out hypocrisy, and speaking truth to power, despite even the most dire of consequences. You may feel like John: misunderstood misfit within God's community, who was even accused by other religious leaders of having a "demon."[1] Perhaps you notice that sometimes, like John, you attract people who are drawn to your power—people who only want to be entertained or feel better rather than sincerely follow Jesus.

Jesus was really impressed with John. One day, He confronted the crowds, asking if they had gone out into the wilderness to see a rich leader in comfortable clothes, someone who could be easily swayed by popular opinion. Obviously not. So, Jesus asked, "What then did you go out to see? A prophet? Yes, I tell you, more than a prophet. ... Truly, I say to you, among those born of women there has arisen no one greater than John the Baptist."[2] How did this Eight become so great? John revealed his secret when asked about the identity of Jesus: "He must increase, but I must decrease."[3] He fully embraced his supporting role as the forerunner to Jesus, preparing the way for someone greater.

Unlike John, unhealthy Eights want to be the big shot. They drink their own Kool-Aid, believing themselves to be indispensable—to their cause and those around them. They make a lot of noise and seek to dominate using provocative language, money, charisma, or through sheer force of will. They may try to build their own earthly kingdom by acquiring more properties, businesses, or followers to reach for a higher degree of immortality. The more unhealthy and insecure they are, and the more powerless they feel, the bigger they must become.[4]

> Your destiny can be etched into the minds of future generations too.

Healthy Eights, however, declare with pride, "I must decrease." Look to the legacies of fearless figures like Joan of Arc, Frederick Douglas, Sojourner Truth, William Wilberforce, Mother Theresa, Cesar Chavez, and Dolores Huerta. Their commitment to selflessly champion a cause beyond themselves propelled them into the archives of history. Your destiny can be etched into the minds of future generations too, if you steer the world's gaze beyond yourself toward the mission of Jesus.

---

1   Matthew 11:18
2   Matthew 11:9,11a
3   John 3:30
4   Riso and Hudson, *The Wisdom of the Enneagram*, 301.

The Good News for Defenders is you can become great even if you don't accomplish your big vision. An Eight knows, "If I die, I die. But the vision will live on." Think about the tragic endings of Jesus, John the Baptist, or a modern example like Martin Luther King Jr. Their lives were cut short, and they couldn't see the finish line of their own hopes. John would not live to see Jesus rise from the dead. Martin Luther King Jr. preached about how he would not make it to the promised land but that he had "been to the mountaintop." Their vision lives on in those they have inspired.

Even if you feel like you haven't done enough, you don't have to see your dreams fulfilled to leave your mark on the world. Eights make such an impression on others that even through their death they can inspire a multitude of followers to carry on their work, accomplishing impossible things for the glory of Jesus and to honor what you started.[5]

No guilt in life, no fear in death
This is the power of Christ in me
From life's first cry to final breath
Jesus commands my destiny
No power of Hell, no scheme of man
Can ever pluck me from His hand
'Til He returns or calls me home
Here, in the power of Christ, I'll stand.[6]

→ Pray

Father, I'm humbled by the life of John the Baptist, a great leader who lived to make much of Your Son, Jesus, not himself. Show me how to play a supporting role in the grand narrative of Your redemption, recognizing that my contributions, no matter how big or small, can resonate for generations to come.

---

[5] Riso and Hudson, *Personality Types*, 307-308.

[6] Keith & Kristyn Getty – "In Christ Alone." Genius, January 1, 2006. https://genius.com/Keith-and-kristyn-getty-in-christ-alone-lyrics.

Day 40 Reflections:

In what ways do you identify with John the Baptist's fearlessness and commitment to truth-telling in your own life?

How can you discover a sense of fulfillment, understanding that your vision, despite remaining unfinished, can leave a lasting legacy in the world?

How do you want the world to remember you?

> ### → Respond
>
> Find a life coach, spiritual mentor, or counselor to come alongside and support you in accomplishing your goals. Start working courageously toward something today that seems impossible without God's supernatural power and grace.

Prayer for Defenders

Father, I am deeply grateful to You for creating me in Your image as Your beloved child. You created me specifically to reflect Your power and strength. Thank You for the times You have led me to get necessary things done, to defend the people and causes I love, and for the will to relentlessly pursue justice. I confess that my need for intensity has often led me to burn out or burn bridges with others. I have found myself being excessive, insensitive, impulsive, and rebellious at times, but You, being rich in mercy, saw me from heaven and sent Your life-giving Son, Jesus, to die on the cross when I was burdened with guilt and at my weakest. Now I revel in the fact that I can completely trust in You. I can rest, knowing You will never betray me and will defend me against all my enemies. Clothed with the power of Your Holy Spirit, I will embrace vulnerability as an asset, remembering that when I am weak, I am strong. Putting off my tough, invincible self, and putting on my new, innocent self made in Christ's image, I will make my mark on the world by pursuing mercy over revenge, empathy over ego, and resting in God's presence before springing into action.

Three Types of Defenders

Below is a summary of the three types of Eights (called subtypes) from the teaching of Beatrice Chestnut, whose book, *The Complete Enneagram*, covers all twenty-seven subtypes of the main nine Enneagram types.[1] As discussed in the introduction, these subtypes help us drill down the different nuances of the Defender.

Warning: many of these descriptions will seem overly negative. However, one of the main purposes of the Enneagram is to help us discover our "shadow self"—the ways we interact with the world unconsciously and in times of stress. These descriptions are not indictments; rather, they are a further opportunity to deepen our awareness of how we naturally interact with the world and ways to make healthier choices for ourselves and those around us.

The Self-Preservation Eight

The Self-Preservation Eight is the epitome of a no-nonsense person. Direct and productive, this type has a quiet strength that draws others under their protective wings. These survivalists know how to bring home the bacon, get what they and those around them need, navigate difficult situations, and protect their investments. They have an intolerance and frustration—both which mask a fear—around not getting their material needs met. They are businessmen and women who know how to barter, bargain, and get the upper hand. Stoic and less expressive than others, they express no pretenses, no fusses, and give no long explanations. This subtype is the most "armed" and self-protected of the Eights and may display an exaggerated selfishness, independence, materialism, or territorialism. While all Eights are prone to revenge, this subtype may desire it without knowing exactly why. They are more private and less charismatic than the other subtypes due to their innate self-containment and occasional undervaluing of emotions (which may cause them to look like Fives). This Eight can also be confused with a One-to-One One, who also has a drive to get what they want above all else, but while Ones still observe social norms, Eights go against social conventions (often intentionally) and may make up their own rules.

---

1   Chestnut, *The Complete Enneagram*.

The Social Eight

The Social Eight is the "countertype"—quite literally, the one whose actions often run counter to the archetypical Eight. They are friendly, supportive, service-minded, and less quick to anger. However, as they are extremely sensitive to exploitation, they can, like all Eights, become very assertive and aggressive while protecting others. This Eight's rebelliousness is manifested by challenging the dominant culture or oppressive authorities, often with expressive/prophetic acts of disobedience. This high level of activity may lead them to lose themselves in constant motion. These Eights love the influence they can have within a group, but if their pride is not kept in check, can come to see themselves as more indispensable, powerful, or famous than they really are. The community may be prioritized over individual relationships as they unknowingly replace their need for love and intimacy with one or two people with the satisfaction that comes from leading or being part of a group. Valuing honor and trust above all, they will go to the moon for those in their inner-circle but may feel betrayed and hold grudges more easily than other Eights. They are charming visionaries and storytellers, but when unhealthy, they may make promises they don't follow through on. Male Social Eights are often confused with the calmer Type Nines and Female Social Eights with the ever-helping Type Twos. The "tell" is that Eights tend to act in more direct, powerful ways, engaging more readily in conflict as they protect the less powerful.

The One-to-One Eight

The One-to-One Eight is passionate, outspoken, surprisingly emotional, and openly rebellious. They seek out pleasure, adventures, risks, challenges, and love the thrill of the chase (but lose interest if they win too easily). They like to play rough and are stimulated by a good debate. These Eights often take on mentoring roles and intentionally seek to have a major impact on the lives of those in their sphere of influence. Being the most anti-social Eight, they provocatively go against the grain and demonstrate just how different their ways are from the norm. Nevertheless, their magnetism and charisma result in natural leadership abilities and help them capture people's attention. More than gaining material security or approval, they like to dominate and exercise power over others and may see everything in life as an object to possess. In romantic relationships, these seductive Eights are life-giving and energetic but may get jealous or abusive when unhealthy. This subtype fits the most common description of an archetypical Eight but may be confused with One-to-One Fours, who can be angry, emotional, and demanding. However, one difference is to see that, while Eights are inherently confident and assume leadership naturally, Fours suffer from a deep-felt sense of deficiency, which results in a more retiring personality.

Next Steps

I'm so proud of you for finishing this 40-day journey. That's a big accomplishment! Though this book isn't small by any means, you may feel (like me) that we've only begun to explore the tip of the iceberg. You're probably wondering: *What now? My eyes have been opened, I've grown in greater self-awareness and empathy, and now I'm ready to take the next step!* Here are some ideas:

1. Follow "Gospel for Enneagram" on Instagram, YouTube, Facebook, or Twitter to continue learning and engaging.

2. Download my free resource called *Should Christians Use The Enneagram?* at gospelforenneagram.com.

3. If you found this book helpful, please leave an honest review (or star rating) online or share on social media so others can find it.

4. Visit my website, gospelforenneagram.com, to find more helpful links and resources.

5. Join a church community where you can continue to grow in your knowledge of God and self. To go the distance, find a mentor, coach, or support system.

6. Ask a friend, spouse, or mentor to meet regularly with you to discuss the insights God has revealed to you through this book. Invite them, along with your small group, to get a devotional on their Enneagram type and share what they learn with you.

7. Email me with any thoughts, questions, or feedback to tyler@gospelforenneagram.com. I'd love to hear from you!

Acknowledgements

My wife: Lindsey, you show me the gospel every day by loving me for who I am and not what I do. Thank you for your tremendous encouragement to be a writer and for bearing with my workaholic tendencies. I want to be more like you.

My editors: Joshua, thank you for bringing your incredible creativity to the table. Your re-rewrites helped elevate my writing to a whole new level. Stephanie, your attention to detail and passion for this project gave me tremendous confidence. Lee Ann, your veteran experience and thoroughness increased the value of this book tenfold.

My coach: John Fooshee, thank you for your Enneagram coaching and partnership. I'm deeply grateful for your willingness to come alongside me and put wind in my sails.

My influences: I wouldn't have been able to pull this off without a multitude of direct and indirect influences such as pastors, teachers, and writers (including you, mom!) over the years. I'm deeply grateful for the spiritual heroes who have come before me and shaped me.

www.GospelForEnneagram.com

Follow us:

 /GospelForEnneagram

 @GospelForEnneagram

 @GospelForGram

 Gospel For Enneagram

INTRODUCING

A DEVOTIONAL SERIES WITH SPOT-ON TRUTHS FOR YOUR TYPE.

Improver **Helper** **Achiever**

Individualist **Investigator** **Loyalist**

Enthusiast **Defender** **Peacemaker**

GET NEW BOOK UPDATES AT
GOSPELFORENNEAGRAM.COM

Made in the USA
Monee, IL
18 December 2023